F*CK
FEARLESS
Making the BRAVE Leap

Praise for *F*CK FEARLESS: Making The Brave Leap*

"Heather Vickery's approach to redefining what it means to be brave, every day, and how that can change your life in magical ways, is a game-changer! Read this book, put it into practice, and then share it with everyone you know."

- Aaron Anastasi, author of The Voice of Your Dreams and Your Prosperous Mind, Actor and Coach

"The past few years have been difficult for many and we've had to fight the age old need to pull ourselves up from our bootstraps and get through it. Heather's book is a refreshing take on bravery, stress, and realizing that fearlessness doesn't exist for many. It's working through, knowing the fear isn't going anywhere that shows us what we're really capable of. Heather's book is a must read for those who have felt shamed for their survival story, for those who have been silent because their fight doesn't look like someone else's."

- Christina Garnett, Community Builder and Advocacy Strategist

"A successful millionaire told me as a newbie entrepreneur that fear never really goes away. I was disappointed until I realized that she was right. The absence of fear is NOT the goal. Heather's book spoke to me the same way. Why expend our precious life-force on trying to eliminate fear when we can be brave instead? This approach is a must-read for everyone with a big dream in their heart."

- Denise Duffield-Thomas, Money Mindset Mentor and author of Chill & Prosper

"I remember years ago someone asking me who I wanted to be when I grew up. I said, 'Unapologetically me.' The problem was, I didn't know how to show up bravely. That's because my definition of bravery was wrong. F*ck Fearless has changed that perspective, unraveling tight definitions that constrict us and unpacking new approaches to free us. These new thought patterns, action steps, and mindset shifts are changing the way I approach hard situations that previously would've rooted me in fear, causing me to stop moving forward. I can't recommend this book enough."

- Kimberly Crossland, CEO and Founder of Cruisin' + Campfires

"Some people take leaps of faith, Heather Vickery takes leaps of purpose. The power of her intention is palpable in the pages of her book, F*ck Fearless. This is a book that challenges you to do what you know you should do—to take charge of your life with grace and grit. This is a book to share with your circle. Just be sure to tell them to buy their own copy, because you're going to want to re-read yours."

- Lorraine Schuchart, APR, Disruptive Brand Strategist and Founder, Prosper for Purpose

"So often we end up with life happening to us, instead of being intentional about making life happen for us. In F*ck Fearless, Heather not only helps readers take empowered action, but gives specific, "BRAVE" actions to take in every area of your life so you don't end up 10, 20, 50 years down the line wondering what happened to you and why you never really "went for" your dreams and goals. Such a great read and so valuable for anyone who's ready to make life happen for them!"

- Yael Bendahan, Marketing + Mindset Coach

F*CK FEARLESS
FEARLESS
Making the BRAVE Leap

HEATHER VICKERY

 **Four Little Birds** PUBLISHING

First Edition

For permission requests, write to the publisher, c/o Heather Vickery, addressed "Attention: Permissions Coordinator," to heather@vickeryandco.com.

The opinions expressed by the Author are not necessarily those held by Four Little Birds Publishing.

Ordering Information: Quantity sales and special discounts are available on quantity purchases by corporations, associations, and others. For details, contact the publisher at the email address above.

Edited by: Sabrina DelMonaco and Lee Lee McKnight
Cover design and layout by: Jessie Leiber

Printed in the United States of America.

ISBN: 978-1-7336185-3-3

Library of Congress Control Number: 2021917887
First edition, October 2021.

The fonts used are Paris Dreamer, Baskerville, and Poppins.

I've often wondered why people name the fonts used in their books. It seemed such an odd practice to me. Until I was selecting fonts for this book. It, somehow, became a very personal and difficult decision. I struggled to decide which fonts to use based solely on appearance. And that's when I learned that the beautiful brushstroke font used in the books is called "Paris Dreamer." That was a sign from the universe! As you'll soon discover, having a home in Paris is something I'm actively manifesting. As you read through this book, and move through your life, I hope you're always open-minded to seeing the signs in whatever unique way they present themselves. - HV

To Olivia, Eve, Tessa and Scarlett for showing me the path to bravery. Thank you for believing in my ability to change the world.

Love, Momma

Contents

Legacy and Intention

"If you hear a voice within you say 'I cannot paint,' then by all means paint and that voice will be silenced."

— VINCENT VAN GOGH

I started writing this book in early November 2020; in fact, as I write this preface, it's Election Day in the United States. I suspect that date may mean something to you by the time this book is in your hands. Today, I feel especially vulnerable because this election holds our future in its hands like no previous election ever has.

This might be a strange way to start a book about making brave choices, but I'm sharing this so you know that I wrote this book during one of the most stressful and wild times in modern American history. If I'm honest, this book has been a lifeline for me—a healthy distraction from the trauma of the election and the preceding years of political angst. And perhaps it's a little about making my mark in history and helping you do the same. I've been looking inward, asking myself, "Who do I want to be in the world?" and "What type of impact do I want to make?"

I want you to think about these questions for yourself as you begin this book. The journey of this book is about getting to know yourself, figuring out what you really and truly want, and then *making it happen.*

And, well, I guess what I want to impart to you is this: Writing this book was hard, and it was stressful—because writing a book *is* hard and stressful—but I can do hard things, and so can you. I hope that by the time you're finished reading this book, you'll realize that the hard things may not always be the expected things. Sometimes the hard things are the small, seemingly insignificant things that heal us, push us, and connect us. Sometimes slowing down is what's hardest. Perhaps it's a pause, a reflection, a moment of grace.

In many cases, we push the hardest things to the side because, at first glance, they don't appear to be important enough. It's time to rewrite that storyline. To redefine how you want to move through the world and what it means to be brave, successful, vulnerable, and empowered.

Writing this book has been a labor of love. It's been building inside of me for years as I dragged myself through my own transformation—one that included coming out (yes, of the closet!), getting a divorce, closing a successful business to launch a new one, and essentially burning it all to the ground and rebuilding it. This time around, however, I built it the way I wanted it, rather than the way society told me it was supposed to be. This time I like my business, and myself, a whole hell of a lot more. I want that for you as well. Because, just like me, you fucking deserve it!

The steps I share in this book helped me begin, again, from the ashes of my burnt-down life. Once I took a step back and realized what got me through the awful stuff and into the awesome stuff, I recognized this process could support others—folks like you—in their transformations. It didn't have a name back then, of course. *Now, I call it The BRAVE Method.*

What are we transforming, you ask? Well, everything. Our hearts, minds, bodies, families, businesses, communities, nations. Everything. When I realized that The BRAVE Method could be applied to every situation, I knew I was onto something big. I then set about doing the work and providing research to prove my case, which I share with you in the pages of this book. You'll read case studies from clients I've worked with, guests I've interviewed on my podcast, and my own personal stories.

For now, in this preface, I want to focus on something a little different because it's still Election Day for me, and I can't help but sit with the concept of legacy and what we leave behind.

Whether you're aware of it or not, you're always creating impact. Always leaving something behind even when you don't realize it. Once you recognize you're creating impact, and lead from there, you'll be far better off, and have more control, because you can be intentional about the impact you create. But it isn't always about what you leave behind, it's also about where you're building from. I want you to love and appreciate where you are right now, at this moment. Your choices led you here. Don't judge those choices, be grateful for them. You are on the precipice of something extraordinary. Use your experience and knowledge to build a foundation of self-love and good (enough) right now. It's from this foundation that good can become great, and great can become wildly amazing. Better off is always better than where we are, even if where we are is fucking fantastic. By being intentional, we only pass down the things we truly want to leave behind.

Someone is always watching and absorbing our message, our energy. I know for a fact that my children are watching and learning. When my youngest daughter was first learning to talk, she would answer "Sure" whenever anyone asked her a question. "Sure" was her "Yes." I thought it was adorable, but I couldn't figure out where she'd learned it. One evening I mentioned it to a friend, who looked at me, shocked. She said, "That's what you say instead of responding 'Yes!'" *What? I do?!* I had no idea.

At that moment, I realized how my daily, often unconscious, behaviors affected and shaped the people around me. My baby responding "Sure" rather than "Yes" wasn't a big deal—but what else was she picking up from me?

I'm fairly self-aware. I know that my big-scale decisions and behaviors leave impressions on my kids and will be a major part of my legacy. But the imprint I leave runs deeper than them seeing me speak on a big stage or publish a book and thinking their mother is 'cool' (I am pleased to say that as of now, they do still think I'm cool). You're always leaving an imprint on the lives of your children and everyone else you spend time with because that's human nature.

In light of this, I urge you to consider a couple of key questions. What type of values do you want to instill? How can you best support others while allowing them to be their own guides? This can apply to literally any situation in your life, be it children, friends, partners, clients, coworkers, or community members. If I'm talking about my kids, my main goal is simply not to raise assholes. But that starts with not being an asshole myself. Sometimes it's a work in progress, but I'm always striving to learn, be more aware, be more intentional, and do better.

Parenting, like entrepreneurship, is intense! We hold these tiny humans in the palm of our hands and the best we can hope for is that they do more, achieve more, and are happier than we could ever imagine. Most of us want our children to be far happier and successful than we believe we're capable of ourselves. I remember my own mother telling me, "I want you to be so much more than me." I used to think that was silly because she was pretty awesome, but I get it now. We want more for our children no matter how much success we've had in our lives. That's the natural way: To want your children to do better and have more than you did.

My first business was an event and wedding planning firm. When I transitioned from that into coaching, I felt wildly out of my lane and extremely unsure how to get where I wanted to go. But I knew enough from the previous eighteen years as an entrepreneur to know that there was no such thing as "I don't know how." When we want to *know* how, we figure *out* how.

I started by having conversations with other coaches I admired. One suggested I host a workshop that was invitation-only to practice my craft and get some concrete feedback. It was both a wildly exciting and terrifying idea. But I embraced it and reached out to several creative thought leaders and business owners. I asked them to join me for a free workshop in return for their feedback and testimonials. To my delight and slight surprise, each and every one of them said they would be thrilled to join me for a test run workshop. Not only did I get to finetune my workshop and coaching skills, but it was an excellent opportunity to learn from each of them—giants in their fields.

That first workshop was truly an exceptional experience. By creating it, I proved to myself that I had something valuable to say, that people appreciated the skills I brought to the table, and that I was respected and worthy. I also got to practice my coaching skills, and there is always value in that. Plus, everyone loved it, and afterward, each of them reached out to thank me. One of them even turned into a one-on-one coaching client!

Several years later, I ran into one of the CEOs who had attended that very first workshop. He spotted me across the room at a fundraiser, gave me a big hug and said, "Heather, I have been in business for thirty years. What I learned from you has completely changed the way I do business."

It turns out, he had implemented some fairly basic boundaries and started to manage his clients' expectations better by being realistic about turnaround times. He was able to change the way he did business and how he felt while doing his job, and it transformed the client experience as well.

I had no idea that my first workshop would create such an impact for such a cool, successful industry leader. It took a lot of courage for me to lead this workshop, but by being brave, I gave myself the opportunity to create self-trust, gain valuable experience, and build relationships that would support me through the years.

Another benefit of leading that workshop was learning a valuable lesson: you never know what will resonate with others. Since then, I've remembered to connect with people even when I didn't know where it would lead to, whether there would be an ensuing profit, or what the value would end up being. The connection itself was valuable enough.

Connection is one of the values that I've implemented in other areas of my life—not just in business. When I made the painful decision to get a divorce, it was so my daughters would see me not settle for a loveless marriage. I want them to seek a full partner in life. When I came out (yeah, that was hard), I wanted them to see me embrace my authentic self and know that whoever they were, whoever they wanted to be, was enough, and they would be loved and accepted for it. When I marched in the Women's March and dragged those little ladies with me, I wanted them to know they are powerful and that their voices make a difference. When I set firm boundaries around my office hours, it's so they know our family time is important to me. I want to build my legacy on those values.

Legacy, such a big word. It's something that we leave behind with or without our permission and, sometimes, with or without our knowledge. For my daughters, I hope to leave a legacy of courage and truth. And that's actually what I'd like to leave behind for you too, my friend. I want you to dream the biggest, most expansive, life-fulfilling, and joyful thing you can imagine and then believe that it can be yours. Take the time to dream, allow yourself the space to imagine the possibilities, and then take small, intentional steps towards achieving the first element of that dream. Own the powerful force you are!

During this election season (which, as I mentioned before, coincided with a pandemic), I campaigned and phone banked—And I took my kids along for the ride. We talked about why it was necessary, and they made phone calls right along with me. I made them all promise that they would vote in every election, big or small, for their entire lives. Because *all* elections matter. Their voices matter. Their involvement matters. Using your voice is a surefire way to gain personal power and control. As long as you embrace that, no one can take your voice away from you—at least not without your permission.

Everything I share with you in this book was hard-learned and filled with struggle. I don't get it right all of the time, but I strive, every day, to be the same person in public that I am in private. I look people experiencing homelessness in the eye—even if I cannot give them anything, I treat them like the human beings they are. I speak up for those that cannot do so themselves. I fight for justice. I offer help to my friends and loved ones when I see they need it. I say "Please" and "Thank you." I practice gratitude daily, as often as possible, and we have a family gratitude share at dinner each night. I do these things when my children are watching and when they aren't. Because it's the right thing to do—and that is the impact and legacy I want to leave my children and the world. It took me a long time to realize these were, indeed, brave acts. But they are brave.

Having integrity is brave.

Asking for what you want is brave.

Keeping your word is brave.

I'll be the first to admit I am far from perfect. There are countless stories of me being on my phone and one of my girls having to call my name multiple times to get my attention. Or having one of my toddler-aged daughters walk up to my laptop, shut it, and say, "Play with me!" Stories like that are a dime a dozen for all of us. Sometimes I don't feel grateful and on occasion, I'm short-tempered and rude. It's human to make mistakes, slip up, fail, or forget. Yet I always have a solid foundation to lean on and return to. When I get off course, I know how to get back on track.

In the end, I hope my four little girls will go out into the world as powerful forces of nature, and as they breathe their essence into everyone and everything they encounter, I hope their souls think, "My mother would be proud." Because I am.

So for my daughters, and for you, I share The BRAVE Method. I know that using this method, with grace and intention, will change you. It will change how you move through the world. It will change how you interact with others. It will give you a sense of comfort and control in a world where there are often meager amounts of both. I know it will change you because it changed me.

Remember, you'll never fully know your impact. Go into any situation assuming it will be significant and plan accordingly. Act intentionally in order to leave the legacy you desire and then, a byproduct is that you create a ripple effect that may just change the world.

How to Use This Book and Why It Matters

"Don't be too timid and squeamish about your actions. All life is an experiment. The more experiments you make the better."

— RALPH WALDO EMERSON

Brave Action Prompts

The BRAVE Method is more than just an acronym. It's a living, breathing entity that adapts according to the choices you make. It can accommodate your life as it is now and as you want it to be in the future, which you'll discover as you complete the Brave Action prompts.

The book is designed to be interactive and actionable. I don't want you just to read the words and think about them. I want you to get into action and begin making your brave leaps! That's why you'll find Brave Action prompts throughout the book.

These prompts will get you straight to work using The BRAVE Method and building a life and/or business you love. You have options here because, let's face it, every day is a 'choose day.' You can either do these Brave Actions as you move through the book or wait until you've completed the book, then go back and do them all at once. What's important is that you don't use the action prompts as a tick-box exercise. Really dig into them! And be sure to come back and do these prompts over and over again. They change and evolve with you, meaning you'll get new, useful insights every time that can be applied and reapplied throughout your life, as many times as you need.

The BRAVE Method is even more fun if you do it with a buddy! Who can you share this book with? Invite them along the journey and help each other stay accountable. Honestly, this work can be hard to do completely on your own, so grab a friend and work your way through this book together.

Brave Spotlights

I love to read about others' experiences. I find it to be so enriching and motivating. Within the pages of this book, you'll find inspiration and encouragement in many forms, including the Brave Spotlights that feature several of my clients, and as well as guests from *The Brave Files* Podcast.

The BRAVE Method, once learned, is an intuitive guiding element. While Brave Action prompts will help you get into action yourself, the Brave Spotlights will show you examples of how others have enacted The BRAVE Method in everyday life and business.

If you're a curious sort, like me, you may want to know even more about the people featured in these Brave Spotlights. The resource list at the end of this book will direct you to the full podcast episodes, where appropriate. It also includes links to any of the resources mentioned throughout the book.

Redefining Bravery

One of my all-time favorite things in the whole wide world is musical theater. I even minored in theater in college. And one of my favorite shows is *Hamilton: An American Musical*. With *Hamilton*, Lin-Manuel Miranda found a way to reach across generations and audiences to connect history, art, and truth in an imaginative and magical way.

Now, I know that it's historical fiction. But you'd be hard pressed to find much out there that isn't, at least in some ways, invented! The thing about history is that it's told by the victors. It's often misshaped, mishandled, and misguided while it finds its way to us. *Hamilton* may not be historically perfect, but the message and movement it created are pretty damn close to being perfect.

When we're creating a movement, we want others to imagine themselves experiencing greatness. You can't be a successful leader unless you inspire and connect. What *Hamilton* did was allow children of color an opportunity to see themselves in pivotal historical roles and imagine themselves in those powerful roles in the future. It spoke to the fact that we must tell our own stories rather than wait for someone else to do it for us.

Own your story, my friend. Own it and share it with the world because no one will tell it the way you do. No one else can tell your truth. That responsibility is firmly on your shoulders.

While there are many quotable lines in the show (and trust me, I can turn almost anything into a *Hamilton* quote), one that resonates with me every time is from the song "Yorktown."

"And so the American experiment begins,
With my friends all scattered to the winds,
Laurens is in South Carolina,
Redefining bravery. We'll never be free until we end slavery."[2]

This isn't a history book. I could have long conversations with you about how 'The American Experiment' isn't and wasn't what we were sold in our high school history classes, but that's not why we're here. This is a book about making the brave leap. So let's talk about bravery. Bravery has long been defined as something massive, a nearly impossible thing that only people with magic skills or super strength can embrace.

When I was a child, bravery always meant BIG things. It meant climbing mountains or moving a car with your bare hands. Bravery wasn't something that we had the opportunity to embrace every moment of every day.

Then, when I became an adult, I heard a lot of people talking about being 'fearless.' This notion that they could do anything without a moment's hesitation or concern. That they were bigger and more powerful than fear. This was a concept often embraced by entrepreneurs. And it starts young! I've heard the statement "She is fearless" many times over while talking to other parents about our little girls on the playground. Why do we do this!? Pretending we're not afraid causes a lot of harm. It allows us to hide from our truths and pretend everything is okay or easy, even when it's not. And it puts extreme, unnecessary, pressure on ourselves and others if we think we're failing by *not* feeling fearless. Well, I say FUCK FEARLESS.

"I say FUCK FEARLESS."

Being fearless is a really stupid goal. If you're truly fearless, you don't pause to consider the consequences of your actions. When you're actually fearless, you walk in the middle of the street because you're positive the cars won't hit you. If you never walk next to fear, you are likely causing harm to yourself and others. Fearlessness is not a place of honesty. It's a place of hiding.

As I grew into myself and started leading from a place of vulnerability and honesty, I learned that fear is a natural human emotion. It can save our lives. There's a pretty good chance that if you walk in the middle of the road often enough, you'll get hit by a damn car!

Fear is, often, nothing more than:
False
Evidence
Appearing
Real.

As my friend and author of *Your Prosperous Mind* Aaron Anastasi says, "Unless you're being chased by a bear at this very moment, fear is *always* in the future."[3] And if fear is in the future, then it's not a clear and present danger. That means you have some control and power over it. You can change the story! If you're pretending to be fearless, then you don't stop to investigate the fear and learn from it. You cheat yourself out of the opportunity to make different, more intentional, and action-oriented choices.

The most important thing to remember is that we can learn from our fears. What are our fears trying to stop us from doing? Is your fear an immediate survival response or something more nuanced like "If I tell my friend their behavior hurts my feelings they won't like me anymore," or "I can't sell my services for this much money! No one will ever pay that much." Those fears, the nuanced ones, are often biased. I refer to these fears as "limiting voices." They are a bunch of bullshit stories your brain is telling you in an effort to "protect" you, when what they're actually doing is keeping you small and feeding into your fears. It's time to quiet those voices because they are limiting you. And you, my friend, were made to live big. You are here, and your voice is valuable.

I've spent a lot of time studying bravery. What it means. How it affects us. How it motivates us. With the creation of my podcast, *The Brave Files*, I've embraced a mission of *redefining* what bravery actually means. For some folks, bravery is as simple as getting up each day instead of giving up. For others, it's sitting with your child as they die or being a surrogate and carrying a child for someone else. Often, it's speaking up for yourself and for others. Bravery is asking for what you want and believing you are worth getting it. Bravery is raising your hand and demanding your seat at the table, or maybe creating your own damn table! For you, bravery may be embracing your authentic truth. For others, perhaps it's rewriting their story and not being defined by trauma or abuse.

One thing we know for sure is that there are a thousand ways to choose bravely each and every day. And when we choose bravely, on purpose, we choose bigger. We have bigger wins and it's all contagious. It's time for "every day bravery!" No matter what your personal brave is, I want you to embrace it, every day.

Day in and day out, I help people leverage their fear into intentional bravery. But what does this actually mean? Mostly, I help them use their fear to recognize that something good is actually on the horizon. Fear is a litmus test. If we're truly scared, we can use that to inform, motivate, and empower. And sometimes, we discover that the things we "fear" aren't really that scary. But we can't do that unless we explore them and deal with knowledge and facts.

Fear either owns you or empowers you. If you don't take the time to understand your fear, to take it apart and learn from it, then the fear wins. It will shut you down. That's unacceptable. You're here because you're no longer willing to let fear, society, or other people's ideas dictate your life. You're here to take fear by the arm and say, "Okay, you can come with me if you insist, but I'm going no matter what."

Fear allows you the opportunity to be brave. And for that alone, fear deserves some props.

You. Are. Brave.

Whatever you want to do—start the podcast, write the book, get married, have a family, start a new business, ask for that raise—whatever it is, you can do it. In this book, you'll find all the tools and resources you need to get started and stay the course (even though the path is winding and it will change often and rapidly). You are not stuck, unless you choose to be. Once you set an intention and map out an actionable plan with short, bite-sized steps, you can and will achieve whatever it is you most desire.

It's okay to be afraid. It's what you do with that fear that counts. Leverage that fear and choose bravely!

SARAH

Brave Spotlight

✳ What feels BRAVE?

When you take the time to acknowledge what feels brave—and when you're honest about *why* it feels brave—you're able to repeat this behavior more often and know why it matters. Take Sarah Humes, one of my podcast guests, for example. Sarah grew up in poverty. Once, as a child, she awoke to rats crawling on her head while she was sleeping. She also, horrifyingly, remembers studying with her father in the living room and seeing rats nests with baby rats in the corner of the room. As you can imagine, these traumatic experiences had long-term effects. Sarah developed a complete and utter fear of small, furry animals that lasted almost her entire life. Her anxiety was so intense that she was afraid to leave her house for fear she may see a rodent or small animal when she went outside.

But at one point in her life, Sarah realized life was passing her by. The fear and anxiety were winning, and she was no longer willing to accept this. So she took matters into her own hands! A friend had a chinchilla, and Sarah arranged to hold it (We have the video up on the podcast website. It's a pretty incredible moment to watch).

As Sarah faced her biggest fear and held the chinchilla in her hand (in front of her children, no less) she realized that the simple act of leaving her house or holding a small animal was the epitome of bravery for her. And by making braver decisions, even small ones, she showed her children what it means to be brave. And bravery is contagious. ✳

Brave Action

Understanding Your Own Brave

List out all of the things you do that feel brave. It doesn't matter what's on the list, and it doesn't matter if someone else would deem these acts brave. All that matters is that they feel brave to you!

Then, write out *why* these actions feel brave to you.

Finally, write out how you feel after you have completed these brave acts.

No one gets to decide what your brave choices are. Having lived different experiences, we come from different places on the journey. There are a thousand different ways to choose bravely each day.

Own your brave!

The Power of Intention

Picture this, if you will: I was sitting in a crowd of ten thousand people, and Oprah was taking the stage as the keynote speaker. *I was in the room with Oprah!* I knew this experience was going to be life-changing—I mean, it was OPRAH. She was there to talk about the concept of breakthroughs. She shared that her most incredible breakthrough was discovering the importance (and power) of intention. Apparently, the first couple of episodes of *The Oprah Show* were precisely the opposite of what she wanted them to be. This was because, she said, she hadn't bothered to understand what she wanted from the show and what her guests' motivation was for coming on.

She went on to say that the experience led her to choose intention at all times. "There's nothing I do without knowing why and being intentional about it," she said. This applied to what she ate, wore, who she interviewed, where she lived and traveled—literally every element of her life. Of course, it's inspiring to hear someone like Oprah share this story, but we all take it with a grain of salt. From the outside, it appears easy to be grateful when you have everything, which we all assume Oprah does. But I was struck when she said, "You might think I have the privilege of being intentional because I'm Oprah, but I'm here to tell you, I'm Oprah because I choose to be intentional." She then closed by saying, "However amazing you think my life is, it's a thousand times more amazing than that."

> *"You may think I have the privilege of being intentional because I'm Oprah, but I'm here to tell you I'm Oprah because I choose to be intentional!"*
> **- Oprah Winfrey**

This, my friends, is what I want for you. I want your life to be intentionally amazing. This book and The BRAVE Method will help you achieve this. Being intentional in every element of your life—work, family, social interactions, community, and self—will help you maximize your time and be successful in your endeavors. Intentional time weaves a stronger, more efficient structure throughout your life. It's the kind of structure that affords freedom, peace, rest, and control. The kind of structure that sets you free.

I want you to have your Oprah moment. But to get there, you have to be dedicated, focused, and incredibly intentional. You'll need to understand why you want it, why it matters, and why you're taking these specific actions to get there.

You are *worth* the time.

You are *worth* being intentional.

PASHA

BRAVE Spotlight

✳ Healing with Laughter

When it comes to being intentional about how you show up in life, Pasha Marlowe has the market cornered. After nearly losing her son to chronic illness, Pasha made the intentional decision to use humor to survive. She had reached a point where she needed to find a way to live, or else she would die—and she wasn't ready to die. Instead, Pasha, a trained improv professional, therapist, and coach, learned to find levity in heartbreaking and traumatizing situations. She did it so she and her son could push through the tough moments and find some light in the middle of extreme darkness. Laughter provided a distraction from their current reality and even served as a pressure release valve for all of the heavy emotions they were carrying. And while her situation continues to be tough, the way she deals with it is better because she brings humor in whenever possible.

Once she realized how impactful humor and laughter were for her, Pasha knew she wanted to help other people find those things as well. Thus her coaching program ROAR was born. I had the privilege of working with Pasha and participating in her ROAR program as I wrote this book. I choose to intentionally challenge myself in order to advance my own speaking skills. I've always been comfortable on stage, but I've never really used authentic humor when speaking. By bringing in laughter and comedy to connect the pain and hurt from my past into the truth of my today, I'm able to bring that authenticity onto the stage more readily.

I also had Pasha on *The Brave Files* podcast because I knew her story would help others learn to heal their own trauma and heartbreak with laughter. It is only through serious intention, thought, planning, and practice that we're able to heal ourselves with laughter, connect with others on painful topics through humor and find the funny in what would otherwise be terrifying. ✳

Brave Action

What are you afraid of?

This is a great time to sit down and reflect on the things we spend most of our lives avoiding: our fears. Take a moment, right now, to list out all of the things that you're afraid of. You'll notice that some of them are well beyond your control. But with most of them, you'll realize there *is* something you can do to create change, get answers, or feel more confident. The real trick here is being 100% honest with yourself when you do it.

Once you've made your list of fears, go through them one by one and decide what small, intentional, actionable step you can take to create some shift or change in the situation. If you discover there's nothing you can do about whatever it is, perhaps you'll consider letting your anxiety around it go. You can also choose to be ambivalent about it. Sometimes the greatest form of resiliency is in deciding something has no power over you.

But, you see, even in the instance of "There's nothing I can do about it," the act of letting go or choosing not to feed into the fear is an intentional action. With every "Yes" and with every "No," you are making a choice. *Be sure the choices you're making are the ones you actually want to make.*

You Don't *Have* to Do Anything

Several years ago I had a life-changing conversation with my then seven-year-old daughter, Tessa. I was running around getting the kids ready for school. Feeling overwhelmed and stressed, I shouted, "We NEED to leave the house by 8:30!" to which she replied casually and annoyingly calmly, "Why?"

WHY!? Who did this kid think she was? Why did we need to hurry and leave on time? I was so frustrated! I really wanted to reply with "Because I said so!" but I am an advanced enough parent to know that line doesn't actually work. So I told her why.

Me: "We need to leave on time because you and your sisters need to get to school and I have work to do!"

Tessa: "Why do you need to do work?"

Me: "Well, I have to work so that we have food to eat, a place to live, and all of the other things that are important in life."

Tessa: "Yeah, but Momma, you don't *need* to do those things. You *want* to do them! You want to feed us because you love us and don't want us to die. But you don't NEED to."

COMPLETE. STOP.

She was right, of course. And it's such a simple concept! But it's hard as hell to grasp and even more difficult to put into practice. Tessa and I spent some time talking through things that I felt might be needs and she was able to find the want in each and every item. My second grader had just completely schooled me in an area I was supposed to be an expert in. Talk about out of the mouths of babes!

What was most profound about this conversation (besides the fact that my kid is wicked smart) was that once I stopped feeling the pressure of "need" and "should" and started using the word "want," I felt like a totally different person. I communicated with my family and my kids better because I was thoughtful and intentional in my requests and my actions.

Little kids ask "Why?" all the time. They say it so often that we, on occasion, want to throttle them. But perhaps they are not asking for the mechanics of why, but rather the motivation behind it. And we'd all be better served if we take the time to do things because we want to, because we want what's on the other side of action. The truth of the matter is you don't need to do anything. You do things because you want to, or at least because you want the desired result of having done the thing.

Motivation can be a tricky thing. What motivates us (and when it motivates us) can shift, sometimes moment by moment. I have conversations with clients about their lack of motivation all the time, and my key to supporting them is to find the "want" behind the perceived need. While this seems like a fairly easy concept, it's often difficult to put into action because the stories we tell ourselves *about* ourselves get in the way. We're going to talk more about those stories and limiting voices later in the book.

I often find myself working with clients that are in a rut, struggling to run their business effectively because they lack motivation. Everything feels like a "need to do" rather than a "want to do." If this is where you are, you are not alone. A few years ago, my company conducted a survey of over three hundred entrepreneurs and found that 83% of respondents struggle with a lack of motivation at least some of the time.[5]

The word motivation actually has two definitions. The one most people think of is "The desire and willingness to perform a task," but the other definition of motivation comes into play as well and has a lot more power behind it. It's "The reason or reasons one has for acting or behaving in a particular way"—basically, finding the want in any situation.

People who want to take action and get motivated often focus on unsticking themselves from whatever's keeping them from doing what they "need" to do. I'm suggesting that finding the *want* behind the need might be enough to propel you forward.

If you were one of my clients right now, we'd be discussing what is blocking you from having the life and career you desire. This is an important part of the process. Identifying the background noise helps you find clarity about why you're feeling unmotivated and work past limiting beliefs. But this is not enough on its own!

The next time you feel unmotivated, channel your inner toddler and ask yourself "Why." What about this task is dragging you down? Why don't you want to do it? The real key here is this: You *have* to be honest with yourself when you answer. And then, once you've identified why you're avoiding said task, ask yourself what's on the other side of this task. What can you achieve or unlock by doing the thing you're avoiding? Essentially, how badly do you want the desired result?

Each and every one of us lacks motivation at some point. What matters is what you do with the emotions surrounding it. Do you let your feelings take over and keep you from doing the work you were created to do, or do you take steps to uncover why you're feeling unmotivated, what you really want, and how to push through to the other side?

Anytime you hear yourself say, "I need to do this," I challenge you to stop, take a moment, and identify why you might *want* to do it instead. You'll soon discover that you're achieving more, that those achievements are more meaningful and in line with your goals, and that you're better able to communicate your needs to others. This gets other people on board faster and moves you more rapidly to your desired results.

So let's kick the words "need" and "should" to the curb and re-place them with "want!" As one of my clients, Angela, would say, "Stop shoulding all over yourself!"

KHIM

—

Brave Spotlight

✳ Proof of Life

Khim Baggett was one of the earliest guests on *The Brave Files* podcast. When she was thirty-five, Khim was diagnosed with breast cancer. Shortly thereafter, she discovered she was pregnant with her third child. Before finding out she was pregnant, Khim was sure cancer would be the end of her. She was already, mentally, preparing to say goodbye to her loved ones. But pregnancy changed everything for Khim. In our interview, she shared her incredible story of facing both death and life at the same time.

Something shifted for Khim when she found out she was pregnant. Seeing her baby's heartbeat in the doctor's office gave her a renewed sense of purpose. That moment redefined bravery for her. For Khim, hearing her baby's heartbeat was "proof of life"—both for herself and her unborn child. In an instant, Khim knew that she and her unborn child had to beat the odds and not become a statistic—and they did!

Khim is a living example of my firm belief that we don't *have* to do anything. Doctors wanted her to abort her baby to save her own life. They made it very clear that choosing to stay pregnant would, very likely, kill both her and her unborn child. But Khim wasn't having it. She recalls saying, "You're worried about death, I'm worried about life." The desire to fight for her unborn child changed the game. Her battle is a true testament to both physical and mental strength. Rather than live a life in dread—which, to be fair, is an understandable emotion for such a hard time—Khim chose to use her forthcoming child's future as motivation. Getting through cancer treatments wasn't just about beating cancer. It was about preserving life.

Khim finished radiation treatment in October 2017 and had reconstruction surgery the following year. And on the day our interview aired, the baby she carried during cancer treatment turned one.

Every medical case is different, and this Brave Spotlight is not a medical suggestion. Each of us must, always, do what we believe is best for ourselves. That's especially important when it comes to our health and our own bodies. But what I love about this story is that, in the end, it boiled down to Khim knowing what was right for her. She knew her own truth and strength and refused to let others tell her she *had* to do anything. Knowing yourself and trusting your instincts can save lives. ✲

Brave Action

Removing "Need" and "Should"

"Stop shoulding all over yourself!"

One of the bravest things we can do is become deeply and acutely aware of our habits, patterns, and behaviors. Every time you say (or even think to yourself) that you "need to" or "should" do something, you shut yourself down a little bit. No one wants to do what they need to or should. It doesn't feel good and it's not much fun.

For this Brave Action, I want you to start being aware of how often you say "need" and "should." The magic of awareness is that your patterns and habits will shift naturally—that is, without you taking any major steps to eradicate the behavior.

You can keep a list, if you'd like, of how often you say "need" and "should." And then begin to notice when you catch yourself. Do you let this nagging stay with you, or are you reframing the conversation in your mind?

Once you're aware of this pattern, I want you to think about the why behind the need/should. What is possible if you did the thing you don't want to do? What happens when you reframe a need or should into a want?

Reframing examples include:

- I want to make those five sales calls because I know I can change the lives of others if I can show them the possibilities.

- Giving a fifteen-minute warning before the kids transition into a new activity, like leaving the house, will help everyone feel more prepared and less rushed.

- Setting aside twenty minutes to take a walk will allow me to think clearly, feel connected to my body, and prepare me for an effective and productive day.

- Folding and putting away the laundry will help me feel less chaotic and cluttered. It's worth doing so I can feel these things.

- Having an uncomfortable conversation will free up emotional and mental space from something that takes up way too much of my time right now. Results will be better if I bite the bullet and make the call.

Do You Know Who You Are?

The movie *Moana* was released just as my youngest was turning four. As so many children were, she was completely enamored with the movie, and I was perfectly okay with that. If you're not familiar with Moana, she's smart and strong-willed. I think she's a truly great role model for young children. For months, after we'd dropped her sisters off at school and were on our way to daycare, Scarlett would request the *Moana* soundtrack. Because I'd get to listen to one of my favorite musical geniuses, Lin-Manuel Miranda, rap, I never really minded the constant repetition. But inevitably, my favorite moment was when the song "I Am Moana" would come on. The song opens with Moana's grandmother singing and encouraging her to step into who she truly is. The lyrics move me to tears every time I listen.

I've listened to these lyrics over and over. I have written them down and said them out loud. They connect so deeply with me because there is always the potential for our journeys to leave a scar. We cannot know the future in front of us, yet we must still soldier on. We must practice resiliency every single day, even when the road ahead is windy and unclear and the skies gray. When you utilize The BRAVE Method, you don't always have to know what's ahead. You can be confident in yourself and your systems and know that, no matter what, things will be okay.

Listening to "I Am Moana" reminds me of my own transformation. The journey was terrifying. On the outside, I had the picture-perfect American life, with money and privilege and all the good things we were supposed to covet. But inside, I was broken, and I didn't want to hurt others. Upending your entire life is not a light or easy decision. I wasn't entirely sure who would support me or if I was even making the right decisions. Eventually, however, the option to hide myself and my truth was far more painful and had more severe consequences than playing along in a life that didn't belong to me.

When I *knew*, in my heart and soul, that it was time to start coming out, I did it bit by bit. I remember coming out to my friends, one at a time, and each time it literally hurt. The terror was palpable. I felt heavy in my chest and my neck would grow hot. I struggled to breathe. I knew coming out would be difficult and painful, not just for me but for those I loved. However, throughout it all, I truly and deeply believed that what was on the other side was worth it. And then I began to notice something really fascinating. The more I spoke my truth the easier it became to breathe. Each truth allowed a little more air to enter my lungs until I finally felt like I had taken the first deep breath of my life. I didn't even know I couldn't breathe.

I am one of the lucky ones. I know that living a radically authentic life and speaking your truth comes with real danger for some people. Although I feared being harmed or rejected by friends and loved ones, I wasn't. Nearly everyone I encountered accepted my truth as the truth and moved on. When I was far enough removed from the freshness of the experience, I felt myself flush with gratitude. By being vulnerable and presenting my true self to the world, I had given others the chance to really love and support me. And, for the most part, they did. If you don't give people the chance to step up and love you in your authenticity, how will you ever know what is possible?

I chose the empowering side of fear. It was the birthplace of The BRAVE Method. Everything we want is just on the other side of uncomfortable, and let's face it: Fear is extremely uncomfortable. So I embraced the fear and pushed forward. And yes, the journey left scars.

Over time, those scars began to heal. Now I reveal them to you, one by one. They are my personal map. They mark my life experiences, the lessons I've learned, the things that were brave but did not go well, and those that were brave, exciting, and rewarding. When I speak to you, it is from a place of total truth and honesty. The journey has not always been easy—it often still isn't—but it has been, and continues to be, worth it! Part of being successful with The BRAVE Method is doing the work to know who you are.

> *"The things you have learned will guide you and nothing on earth can silence the quiet voice still inside you."*
> **- Lin-Manuel Miranda**

Listen to that voice. Let it take you to places unknown. How can you ever truly know your limitations if you never try new things? Don't be afraid of the scars; they give you character and experience. They are a byproduct of a fulfilling life.

Brave Action:

Owning Your Achievements

Most often, we are our own worst critics. We live in a society that tells us not to brag, to be humble instead. We think it's cocky or rude to toot our own horns—but it's not!

One of the most famous quotes attributed to heavyweight champion Muhammad Ali is, "It's not bragging if you can back it up." That's exactly what I want you to do in this Brave Action.

Create a list of all your accomplishments from when you were a young child until now. Don't leave anything out! Even the ones that you may think are small or silly. Write them all down. Then, once you have them compiled, go through the list as if you're an outside observer (or have a friend go through them with you). Read each accomplishment as if they aren't your own, and assign one word to *describe the person* who accomplished each thing.

Once you've assigned a word to each achievement, read the list of words aloud to yourself. Those words describe you. They are your words. Now it's time to own them.

Example:

Achievements	Descriptive Words
Graduated from college	Dedicated
Moved to a big city all alone	Fierce
Found my own place to live	Strong-willed
Worked three jobs to get by	Hardworking
Started my own business from scratch	Gutsy
Gave birth to four humans	Powerful
Came out of the closet	Authentic
Got a divorce	Resilient
Started another new business	Adventurous
Created a podcast	Committed
Wrote three books	Brave
Became a keynote speaker	Passionate
Served on several board of directors	Compassionate

Unraveling

Let's get one thing straight: We're all human. And being human means making mistakes—a *lot* of mistakes. There will be times when things fall apart. I don't want you to think that The BRAVE Method is about always being happy or positive, because it's not! Following The BRAVE Method helps you plan for and prepare for this falling apart, and it gets you back on your feet much quicker.

There is one story that still haunts me from time to time. My kids are not into sports (Neither am I, so this works out fine for me), but I put my two oldest in soccer when they were young. I mean, that is what you are supposed to do as a parent, right? Put your kids in soccer (Hint: That is not a parenting rule. There are no fucking rules). From day one, the girls hated soccer. They would cry and beg not to go, but "We were not quitters" and "I had paid good money for that class." So each week we went to soccer.

One afternoon, the girls had to change in the car because we'd come straight from school. They both screamed and cried until I finally snapped. When I say snapped, I really, really snapped. I screamed at the top of my lungs, "SHUT UP! SHUT UP! SHUT UP!" I am not much of a yeller, so they immediately got quiet. Then, in my most stern Mommy Voice, I said, "Sit down, get buckled, and DO NOT SPEAK until I tell you to!" They got buckled, and we drove home in complete silence. We got out of the car, still in complete silence, and walked up the steps to the front door.

Standing on my front porch with my terrified and silent children, it hit me that I had behaved exactly like they had: throwing a tantrum and being unreasonable. I felt terribly guilty, but I was still really mad about the entire situation. I stood there for a minute or so as the girls waited patiently for me to unlock the door. Finally, I got down on their level and looked them both in the eyes. "I shouldn't have said shut up," I said. "Those are not nice words, and if you said them to me, you would be in really big trouble. I'm sorry for yelling." I told them why I was so upset and explained that there are better ways to get what we want and need, but, let's face it, sometimes we get mad and yell. The best we can do is own it and apologize. And soccer sucked. They hadn't wanted to do it in the first place, and I was forcing my own expectations of what's 'right' onto them. That behavior is really shitty, and I needed to own that.

I apologize to my children a lot. We all make mistakes, and I want them to know it's safe to make mistakes with me. We will love each other through it. What counts is what we do after the mistake has happened.

Apologizing is brave.

I'm sharing this with you before I fully break down The BRAVE Method because I want you to know, going into it, that this really can get you through the highs and lows. When you build your life and career with The BRAVE Method, you'll be more prepared and aware of what's happening—what's really happening. You'll plan for the times when things change unexpectedly or your schedule gets derailed for one reason or another. You'll prepare to delegate work to those you trust or rearrange your schedule with confidence because you laid a foundation for such things.

The boundaries you have in place will guide you when things get hard. They will direct you and redirect you. And if they don't, you can change them! That's the beauty of the method—it's all about checking in and making the necessary changes to live your best life and run the best possible business.

The BRAVE Method provides the basic principles for creating, adapting, and getting back on track when things fall apart. I hope you'll view everything with this lens as you move through the book.

Why It Matters

Every speaker, trainer, coach, and leader out there has something to say. They want to tell you how to do 'it' better, smarter, faster. In most cases, they want to tell you how to do it their way.

That's not what this book is about. I am not here to tell you how to do things my way. I'm here to help you think of things in a creative way and how to build systems that allow you to do the thinking for yourself. This book is about showing you how to live a bigger, bolder, braver, and more intentional life.

The BRAVE Method is a system that, when implemented, guides you in the decision making process. This method doesn't bark orders, it invokes deep thinking. It doesn't tell you you're right or wrong, it tells you there's a gray area and space for making mistakes and trying again and doing it on your own terms.

Believe it or not, I am often amazed at just how versatile this method is. In nearly every conversation I have I can utilize one component or another. You'd think, as the creator of the method, it wouldn't surprise me any more but somehow it does.

In this section "Why it Matters," I'll delve into the different ways and reasons that implementing The BRAVE Method can impact your life and business. I hope you'll walk away with a 360 view of just how impactful this method can be and, by the end of the book, how simple it is to implement.

Don't get me wrong, this implementation won't be 'easy' but it is, in fact, 'simple.' Good news though, you can do hard things. You do them every day and I don't even know you, reader, but I have worked with enough people in my career that I can say with certainty that everyone is capable. Whatever you need is already inside of you and for this reason, I can truly say "I believe in you." If I didn't believe in you, I wouldn't have written this book.

Creating "Balance"

One of the reasons something like The BRAVE Method matters so much is because it allows us to truly experience balance. You might be thinking "but wait, does balance really exist?" I believe it does.

I meet people every single day that tell me I'm nuts. That balance is a joke and when we expect to achieve balance we set ourselves up for failure. And I agree that balance, in the traditional way it has always been packaged and sold to us, the notion of having "the whole package all at the same time" is complete and utter bullshit.

But that's not what I believe balance to be about. When you desire the feeling of being balanced, all you're actually looking for is feeling level and harmonious. You want to know that the way you've spent your time and attention is the right choice for you. Much like success, balance is self-defined. It's not the scales of justice. You're not trying to create equality in all of the different elements of your life! You're never going to spend 50% of your time working and 50% in your personal life. It just doesn't work like that! Being balanced is about how you feel at the end of the day, week, month, year. And the only real way to know if you are balanced is to check in with yourself! Call it balance, call it harmony, call it whatever you want but trust me when I tell you it's available to you. But first, you have to decide what it actually means to you, in your own life!

What are your systems for checking in on yourself and deciding if your actions, decisions, and habits got you where you wanted to be in a given day, week, month or year? Understanding this and taking action will help you develop your own sense of balance and harmony.

KRISTIN

———

Brave Spotlight

✳ My Balance Looks So Much Different Than Yours

In my Intentionally Brave Entrepreneur's program we spend a lot of time talking about our feelings. This may not sound like a worthy business approach, but it is. When you disregard how you feel when it comes to work and business then you take the humanity out of it.

Kristin has been a member of the program since early on and she's seen many peaks and valleys in her growth. From thinking she wanted to start an entirely new business to reworking her existing business so it fit better with her personal goals and objectives, Kristin finally recognized that she had a lot more control over her life than she believed she did and that the elusive concept of balance and harmony could, finally, be attainable.

There have been many mindblowing "a-ha" moments through Kristin's work in IBE and her self-awareness is always inspiring to me. So when she had an especially rough few weeks, not that long ago, I was surprised to find her beating herself up in a way that she almost never did.

Upon deep reflection it became clear that Kristin didn't feel balanced. She felt pulled and guilty, especially when it came to caring for herself and her own needs. She couldn't seem to put her finger on the problem and she was increasingly angry with herself for not being able to create more balance and regulation in her life. As you might expect, this bled over into her professional life as well.

Here's something important to know about Kristin, she doesn't half-ass anything. She's a total go-getter who goes all the way in, no matter what. When she took vacation it was for weeks or months at a time. Her family time was focused and she didn't allow work in. Similarly working with clients was a singularly focused and dedicated experience. And somewhere along the way she started to believe if she did follow her natural instincts to go big and hard, she was fucking up her chance to experience balance. She thought that "going all in" was a fault. Turns out this thought pattern sucked the life out of her. She felt heavy. She was disappointed in herself and frustrated about why she couldn't accomplish something that seemed so easy for everyone else (hint, it's not easy for anyone!).

While chatting with her IBE accountability partners, and expressing her feelings about this, someone suggested that perhaps, for her, embracing the "all in," planning for it, setting boundaries around it, and communicating it with others is what might actually create the feeling of balance she so desired.

Because balance is not about how you spend your time, it's about how you *feel* about how you spend your time! Kristin started to think about this. Could it actually be "ok" to lean all the way into her natural behaviors without apology or explanation? Could her happiness and sense of balance and harmony be defined so drastically different from others? The answer is, hell yes it can.

By accepting the ways you're naturally designed to succeed, rather than fighting them to fit into societal norms, you are leading with your own strengths. This is how you redefine words like balance and make them fit for you. It's not one size fits all!

As soon as Kristin saw this as a possibility everything shifted. Her glow came back and so did her swagger. She had everything required to allow herself to feel balanced and harmonious, and it didn't need to look like it did for other people. The biggest adjustment here was learning to allow her difference to be okay and not to feel bad about it.

Don't let anyone tell you balance is bullshit. It's not. You can have it! But remember that you can only have it if you create it on your own terms and in ways that actually fit into your life—not one that was designed for someone else. *

Brave Action

Creating Balance

The key to creating and maintaining balance is in honest time management. The only way you'll achieve balance (remember, balance is about how you feel) is if you plan out your time. Don't forget to schedule in personal time; self-care deserves a spot in your calendar too and besides, when it's on your schedule you're giving yourself permission to take action!

- Start by writing down your top priorities in all areas: work, family, social life, self-care, personal growth, etc.

- Make a schedule of your typical day. Take note of everything from the moment you wake up to the time you go to sleep.

- Look at the things that don't serve your priorities and eliminate them where necessary.

- Start time-blocking your new schedule. Look at the big picture. Schedule when you'll work and when you won't. Time-blocking can be in small increments like 10-15 minutes or large ones like entire days or even weeks (as in Kristin's case).

- Set deadlines for the things you want to accomplish and block off actual time for fun and relaxing activities.

When you start time-blocking the big things, you'll soon be able to schedule out the small things as well. If you stay intentional with your time and refocus as necessary, you'll see a complete shift take place in your life. I've done this myself (while growing a business and raising four brilliant, loud, energetic, sassy, drama centric daughters!) so I know it is possible for you too.

Managing your time is about more than creating a plan and sticking to it. It's about staying tuned in to what's working and what isn't. The most successful people are the ones who know that priorities and workloads shift, and they know to pivot right along with them.

Stop Putting Up with Bullshit

The things you are "tolerating" are, quite likely, ruining your damn life. Tolerance is a word bandied about as if it's positive. It's not. Tolerance provides a general "pass" to that which we don't really like but aren't able or willing to change. Tolerance should never be the goal when it comes to people who are, in some way or another, different from you.

Tolerance has a dark side. When we tolerate violence, or hurtful words, or inappropriate behavior in our communities, tolerance can prove destructive. There are often plenty of elements in our lives that we simply "tolerate." Things we have written off with some type of resignation. An acceptance of something that is not really all that acceptable. Perhaps it's working way more than you're playing or having a cluttered office that prevents you from enjoying your dedicated work space. Maybe it's loved ones not respecting your boundaries or never having time to focus on yourself and your own needs.

In this chapter, when I talk about tolerance, I mean our habit of putting up with or ignoring our own negative thoughts and behaviors, or the thoughts, words and actions of others that are limiting us and keeping us stuck. Whether this bullshit is self-inflicted or coming from another direction, your tolerations might be ruining your life.

Dictionary.com defines the term "tolerate" as "to endure without repugnance; put up with." That means simply accepting something as an unavoidable fact. But that's not what we do here folks. We don't just say, "Oh, okay. That's the way it is and there's nothing I can do about it." There is *almost always* something you can do about any situation. Even if the thing you do is decide to "LET IT GO!" (Imagine hearing me sing this in my best Elsa voice—I do have four princess-loving kids, ya know).

When I personally take the time to stop and think about the things in my life that I simply "tolerate," I realize I allow way too much shit to get in my way. When I say this I don't mean physically, although that giant pile of unfolded laundry does block the pathway from my living room to the kitchen. (So, yeah, maybe there are some physical tolerations that I can do something about.) But what I'm really talking about when I say "toleration allows things to get in my way" is that I allow things that I don't like or enjoy, things I can change or control, to continue to exist and get in my way emotionally and mentally.

Tolerances can be anything from dirty dishes and unwashed laundry to unanswered emails or cluttered inboxes. They can also be clients that don't accept your boundaries (we will be talking a lot more about boundaries a little later in the book), partners who don't give you what you need, or a lack of time for self-care. The list goes on and on.

The problem with tolerations is that, by allowing them, we begin to believe they are problems we're stuck with. We think they're keeping us down and are insurmountable. They are not. The choice is yours. If you're the type of person that gets off on having something to complain about, maybe you secretly like the tolerations. If that's not you, then stop being passive and letting all of the bullshit run your life.

Getting to the meat of tolerations begins with two questions: What is happening in your life that you feel resigned about? What bothers you but you just live with it?

It's time to quit tolerating and take some action! Most of us start the New Year off with excitement, motivation, and highly unachievable resolutions or goals. Then we hit March and April and the disappointment begins to surface. Many of us are confused about our direction, having lost our way in the first quarter of the year. Things were harder than expected. There were roadblocks all over the place.

I can't tell you how many clients come to me feeling overwhelmed, depressed, and lost. The goals they set are sitting on an untouched to-do list. It's not uncommon to feel disappointed at this stage. Many of these feelings stem from the knowledge that no one else is to blame for a lack of focus. Oh sure, we can blame outside factors until we turn blue in the face, but we alone bear responsibility for our growth or lack thereof—and we secretly know it!

These feelings can surface and knock us on our ass at any given point. This is, typically, the point where someone says "NO! I can't take it anymore." They wonder if it has to be like this and they reach out for professional support.

Let me tell you right now, NO—it does NOT have to be like this. But the fact of the matter is until you're there, you're not going to be willing to see things differently.

One of the most impactful things you can do, and a fairly easy way to get started, is to identify what you're tolerating and do some quick "cleaning house." Perhaps in the physical sense, but for sure in the mental and emotional sense!

All too often, we allow the day-to-day routine to take over. This "taking over" is almost done without thought or concern. It's a habit, and most of the time we don't even realize it's happening until we're seeing undesirable results. We all lead full lives. Sometimes that fullness feels exciting, but often it feels busy. Busy is such a nasty word. Allowing yourself to feel "busy" sucks the life out of most things.

I love Sara Cameron's TEDx: How To Turn Busy Into Balance. Society has told us that "busy" means we're important. As if it's a badge of honor. But Sara reminds us that being busy is a choice we make based on bad information.[6] It won't actually give you the fulfillment you desire. It won't bring you closer to friends and family. Busy won't make you happy.

Feeling balanced is what makes you happier. But it takes more work! Busy-ness is a "numbing behavior" that allows us to avoid human behaviors like loneliness, grief, sadness, anger, and fear. We're going to talk about a lot of ways to shut down the "busy" highway you've built for yourself, quiet the noise and create a balance that feels good throughout the book.

The thing about real change and growth: We never actually lean into it unless we're finished making excuses and are ready to call ourselves on our bullshit. The first step is deciding to take your life back, to be the writer of your own story and to no longer be a passenger on this journey. How? By finally deciding that feeling this way is unacceptable.

CHRISTIE

Brave Spotlight

✳ What's the worst thing that could happen?

One of my clients, Christie, was tolerating a work schedule that never allowed her to have the same day off as her husband. He was cranky about it, she missed him and felt guilty. When we started to talk about things that were "bothering" her, this came up pretty quickly.

It was obvious this wasn't a situation she enjoyed, so I asked her what she *wanted* to be reality and she said "I want Wednesdays off!" And then she promptly went into all the reasons it wouldn't be possible to take Wednesdays off. Clients might get mad, she might lose business, she'd get behind in work. Blah, blah, blah. I've heard it all before. So I asked her my favorite question.

"If you told your clients you were no longer working on Wednesdays, what's the worst thing that could happen?" And she went through the list again, but this time we talked about how she could communicate this new boundary and what she could do, preemptively, to ensure that she was staying on top of her work and client communications.

Then I asked her, "What's the best thing that could happen?" And this is where she lit up. She could have regular time with her husband. They could go skiing, cook together, and make some special plans. I could feel her energy shift as she stood on the precipice of possibility with this new option. She was inspired.

In so many cases, the worst thing that could happen isn't even that bad if you're honest with yourself about it. But the best thing is pretty freaking great. And in Christie's case (as in many) it was absolutely worth the risk to set the boundary and see what happened. After all, she could change her mind if a client was going to walk out due to her not working Wednesdays. But then, is that the kind of client she really wanted in the first place?

A couple of days later she called me. A little in shock she said, "It worked. It just worked. No one got mad. No one gave me pushback. They all just said 'Ok. Thanks for letting us know.'"

And there it was, she had what she wanted and the worst part was the fear that came with asking. Turns out the actual asking wasn't a big deal at all. As the late, great Maya Angelou once said, "Ask for what you want and be prepared to get it." I like to add in, ask for *specifically* what you want or you may get it in a way you don't want it at all!

For Christie, all it required was communicating that new boundary to her clients and then *sticking to it* when push came to shove. We get to set the rules and as long as we communicate clearly and manage everyone's expectations. When we do so, pretty much anything can be on the table. ✳

Brave Action

Tolerations

Removing tolerations from your life begins with, like so many other things, awareness. You can't change a pattern or behavior you don't realize exists and you can't remove a toleration you don't know is a problem.

Here's your Brave Action for removing tolerations, getting out of your funk and moving into action. Start by taking a look at what you're tolerating. Now's the time to reflect inward and be honest!

- Ask yourself—What's happening in my life?
- Where do I feel exacerbated, frustrated, discouraged or stuck?
- What is taking up valuable brain space?
- Where has your energy gone – if not directly towards your goal-oriented priorities?

Write out a list of tolerations. Most people take some time with this. It's hard at first to identify ten to twenty areas in your life where you are accepting something less than acceptable!

Now that you've identified some of your tolerations it's time to get really honest with yourself. Which of these items can you do something about right away?

Ask yourself how it will feel with these things no longer hanging over your head or holding you hostage. If the answer, when you ask yourself these truth seeking questions, is "I will feel so much better," then do something about them! Start by writing out the solution to getting rid of the toleration.

Imagine yourself having this list eradicated. How will you feel? How will you behave? How will it affect your loved ones or clients? Sit in the space of knowing it is worthy to remove your tolerations and then begin the work.

Some toleration examples include:

- Unfolded laundry → Fold the laundry and put it away.

- Clients don't respect my personal time → Create a strong boundary around your work hours and clearly communicate it with your clients and hold those boundaries firm.

- Never have any private time for yourself? → Identify when you can carve out time for yourself, put it on your schedule and tell anyone else that needs to know about it (co-workers, partner, kids) that you will not be available at that time.

You hold the power to remove tolerations. You simply have to acknowledge what they are, make a plan for removing them, and then do the thing!

PART ONE

The BRAVE Method

Boundaries

Reassessment, Reframing, Resilience

Action and Accountability

Vulnerability

Expand and Empower

Boundaries

Let me tell you about a little love affair I've been having for many years now. It's a love affair...with boundaries. Yes, you read that right. I'm in love with boundaries and I'm ready to share this love with the entire world! I kept this love affair a secret for a long time but no more. You should know about this awesome, life- changing habit. You deserve to be in on it.

The most successful people out there, the ones who appear to have it *all* together, are in on an amazing secret. They know of something that basically guarantees their potential for greatness and they make it a daily habit. Guess what, so do I!

Dictionary.com defines boundaries as limits that define acceptable behavior. But here's the brave addition to that standard definition—these are YOUR LIMITS! You're in charge here! You get to decide what is acceptable and what isn't. These are *your boundaries!* And they give you permission to say "yes" and "no" at the appropriate times.

Defining, creating, and communicating strong, healthy boundaries is the most empowering action you will take in your life. They are the true secret to success. Boundaries tell others what to expect from you and define what you expect of them. They allow you to communicate what you need and desire. And they are *necessary* in order to operate in the best and most effective way possible.

It's not uncommon for clients to approach me with issues that they have struggled with for what feels like ages. Together we begin working past their blocks only to overturn even more frustrations. A lack of boundaries is almost always the culprit. That's because, without solidified and well-communicated boundaries, there will always be a lack of order. Whether that's mass chaos at work or small frustrating inconveniences, they will always be there. Without boundaries, expectations will not be met, and you will feel exhausted – both physically and emotionally.

What is a Firm Boundary?

Let's be clear—we should all establish boundaries. Boundaries are not just for the boss, they are not just for adults, and they certainly are not for "someone else." *Boundaries are for you!*

For example, one of my strong personal boundaries is not working when I have my kids with me. I am a single parent and am only with my babies 50% of the time. I always try to find the bright side of a situation, the silver lining, so to speak. And one of those bright spots in a divorced household is that you have some time to yourself now and again. I am able to schedule that alone time in any way I choose. I work longer hours, take vacations, read all day, watch movies—whatever I want. And in turn, I choose to be completely present when my kids are with me. I stop working when it's time to pick the kids up from school, don't take evening or weekend calls, meetings or clients. I stay focused on my girls. And, let's face it, when I am working I want to be completely present in that space as well, so it works out nicely. This staying focused and present thing is no joke (I even have "be here now" tattooed on the inside of my left wrist to remind me to stay focused!) and it takes serious boundaries to achieve, especially as an entrepreneur who often feels compelled to work at all hours because society tells me "I'm supposed to."

The one exception, for me, is summer—this is when I'm required to have boundary and routine flexibility—which is extremely important in an ever-evolving and growing existence. It's also why reevaluating boundaries is vitally important. We will talk more about this in the Three R's.

I strive to be intentional about how I spend my time with my kids. That's a boundary I've set with myself and not working when they are with me allows me to stay more focused. This works for me and my family, and it aligns with my values. While the word 'boundaries' sounds constrictive, having firm boundaries actually allows for great freedom. *They provide you with the ability to live your life on your own terms.* With them, you stop living in a consistently reactive state.

A firm boundary doesn't always involve other people. In fact, it could solely be a line you draw with yourself, like mine when it comes to not working when I have the kids with me. Think about how you spend your precious, spare time. Are you scrolling through social media? Maybe you compulsively check your emails. No matter the distraction, setting a firm boundary around these activities will increase your productivity, and overall happiness, in unimaginable ways. Boundaries with yourself may not pop up on your radar, but they are *certainly* of utmost importance in terms of personal freedom. I challenge you to think about the ways in which these kinds of personal boundaries could change the course of your day.

Knowing what a boundary is and why it's important is great, but nothing truly changes unless you *create* boundaries in your own life. Setting up systems that will help you maintain your boundaries is imperative because systems provide clear space for you to do your work and live your life *in the way you desire*. Without them your boundaries won't hold. There are many different systems to help maintain your boundaries. You'll want to consider all of the options depending on your specific goals.

The first step here is in taking intentional time to identify what boundaries are needed. I encourage you to think about "what hurts." Typically, if we're honest about what's harder than it should be, feels terrible, makes us upset, or just doesn't work, these are the areas that most need boundaries.

You create boundaries by putting systems in place. These systems can, and will, look totally different for everyone. But they always instill confidence and allow you to control your time and interactions with others. Boundaries enable you to manage expectations; which makes for smoother relationships, even with yourself.

What are a few ways you can set boundaries?

- Setting concrete work hours (and sticking to them)

- Sending new clients a "welcome" letter explaining your hours, communication policies, and preferred mode of communications

- Ending each work day by creating a list for the next day

- Following the list you created the day before and not allowing distractions to get in the way

- Limiting social media time

- Assigning household chores and a weekly schedule for doing them

- Scheduling in personal time for meals, exercise, and self-care

My favorite thing about boundaries is that they allow you to release guilt. I like to say they are your key to guilt-free freedom because once you set a boundary and then communicate it clearly, you have so much more freedom in your life! If you have a boundary around your work hours and you clearly communicate that with your clients and others, then when that 8:30 pm email comes in you don't have to feel bad about responding the next morning! You are empowered to stick to the boundaries you've set.

One common fear for many is that others won't respect their boundaries. While we'd all love to think we have the will to say no whenever we need to, 55% of respondents to a Vickery and Co entrepreneur survey said they have a hard time saying no.[1] Saying no is essentially setting a boundary on what you will or won't do. The ability to say no is critical when it comes to setting boundaries. Here's the most important thing to remember: In most cases, people will understand and respect your boundaries as long as they know what they are, I promise.

With a little productivity planning, you *can* make establishing these boundaries a daily habit. Before you know it, tasks will be streamlined in ways you didn't realize were possible. You will see the light, and you won't want to turn back!

When it comes to boundaries, it all comes down to communication. You can create the best, most kickass boundaries ever but if you don't clearly and regularly communicate them to others they will never, ever work. People cannot give you what you want if they don't know what it is. You must communicate these boundaries with everyone they impact if you want them to work.

One of my favorite ways to do this is sending out a welcome letter to all new clients and employees outlining expectations (what they can expect of me and what I expect of them). You can do this at home by having a weekly or monthly "family meeting" to clarify each family member's household obligations and schedules.

Clearly establishing boundaries, from the beginning, takes the guessing game out of pretty much anything. They let everyone know where the others stand and are totally game changing. If you don't communicate your boundaries to others, *they will not work*! Communication is the most important aspect of establishing boundaries, and starting relationships with that open communication makes all the difference.

MOLLY

Brave Spotlight

✳ A Balancing Act

I often tell clients they don't actually have to believe that The BRAVE Method works to have it be successful. I don't need you to believe me. I just need you to give it a try. One of the early members of my Intentionally Brave Entrepreneurs program, Molly, has taken this challenge to heart. When she first joined my program she was a new and somewhat fledgling entrepreneur as well as a young mother. Molly knew she was onto something with her business but wasn't quite sure what or how to get there.

I love all my clients but I have a special place in my heart for Molly because she happily and willingly started implementing The BRAVE Method from the getgo and she did it in every way possible. I've never seen someone so willing to try new things, adapt and try again.

When we first met, Molly was getting up at 4:00 am to work before her husband and son woke up and working well into the evenings. She had no real sense of boundaries or balance and was, more often than not, overwhelmed to the point of feeling sick.

But Molly is the kind of person that shows up and gets shit done. She's an "all in" kind of person and while that's a great quality, it can also be detrimental if not properly checked and managed. And, truth be told, she was feeling pretty out of control in most areas of her life. So when I presented The BRAVE Method, she was ready to give it a try. Boundaries, it seemed, were an immediate area for growth. She didn't really have many boundaries and while she was great at building systems for everyone else, implementing systems to streamline her business were a bit lacking.

Getting straight to work figuring out what her pain points were helped clearly and quickly identify some glaringly obvious, missing, boundaries. Of course, these are only glaringly obvious if you take the time to pay attention!

First she started scheduling her time more intentionally and not stopping in her tracks to solve every problem on the spot. Instead of responding to client's text or emails straight away, she created a new system where they filled out a task request form on Asana, the project management tool her company uses. This took some time and patience as current clients were being asked to completely re-work how they communicated with Molly and change doesn't happen overnight. With thoughtful patience, Molly eventually got all of her clients to make their requests or ask their questions via this form which helped her stay on top of the many tasks for each client.

Then she scheduled specific days of the week to focus on each project and clearly communicated those days with her client. The key here was in her communication with clients which allowed her the chance to start honoring time with herself in the mornings and her family in the afternoon and evenings. She also completely recreated her customer onboarding process.

Let's be fair here, Molly is a star student when it comes to The BRAVE Method. In fact, I wasn't sure which section to spotlight her in because she really does take it all to heart and utilize the method in every way possible. But Molly's not perfect. Sometimes things fall apart but she always knows when to start over and try again and she's beating herself up less often than she used to.

And I should mention that since joining Intentionally Brave Entrepreneurs her income has increased more than 1100%. I'm not saying this is the norm, because it's not. But it does prove that

if you put boundaries in place (and stick to them!) The BRAVE
Method can completely change your life! *

Brave Action

Boundaries

Setting boundaries is one of the most important and empowering things you can do in life and in business. Taking a few short minutes to identify where you may want to establish new boundaries, or what adjustments may be required for boundaries already set, can be a game changer. Without setting concrete boundaries you're going to reach burnout more quickly and won't be able to give your best to work or family.

Do you have any boundaries already in place? List them out and then create a list of other ways and places you can set boundaries. Maybe you need to stop answering emails after 5pm. Perhaps it would serve you to take a real lunch break and have some time to yourself in the middle of the day.

Boundaries include, but are not limited to:

- Setting concrete work hours that compliment your life

- Putting an email out of office auto responder on during off hours

- Sending new clients a "welcome" letter explaining your hours, communication policies and preferred mode of communications

- Schedule and commit to "learning" time in your day or week

- Remembering to maintain your health while working, eat well and get up to walk around periodically

- Have a regular day of the week or month to spend with friends, a partner or your kids just having fun

- Ending each work day by creating a list for the next day

- Sticking to the list you created the day before.

Ask yourself the following questioned and write down the answers:

- Write out three boundaries you already have in place

- Are these boundaries working for you? How and why?

- What areas are the most challenging for you?

- What can I start doing, stop doing, do more of or do less of to create change?

Next, commit to three new boundaries to begin immediately.

Consider some of these productivity tips to help you maintain your boundaries (many of which you'll find examples for throughout this book):

- Meditation or visualization

- Batch-tasking instead of multi-tasking
- Setting limits and rewards for completing tasks
- Utilize apps and software to help you be more efficient
- Put limits on social media
- Knowing what and when to delegate
- Celebrating all successes, even the "small" ones
- Having a regular, daily gratitude practice

Remember, your vision may not change but the path changes all the time. As your personal and professional life evolves, your boundaries are likely to shift as well. This is not only ok, it's a natural part of the path to success.

The Three R's: Reassessment, Reframing, Resilience

"R" is, probably, the most important letter in The BRAVE Method. While I urge you to take the entire method to heart, ensuring that you have reassessment, reframing, and resilience at the core of all your actions will create the biggest and most impactful areas of change and growth. In fact, you can't actually do any of the other letters in The BRAVE Method WITHOUT utilizing the R's. This is where the hardest work happens and it's the root that leads to being able to implement the other elements of the method.

When I first started developing The BRAVE Method, "R" was only reframing and I spoke specifically about reframing limiting voices. But as the method began to grow, in my mind and in my coaching practice, I realized we were leaving out some pretty important steps. This is how reassessment and resilience made their debut.

If I wasn't an active participant in the Three R's phases of my business, I might have missed updating the method to include reassessment and resilience. That's *how good* this step is. So let's get into it, shall we?

Reassessment

I firmly believe, no, I don't just believe it, I know, that if you set up consistent and frequent reassessment systems and opportunities, you'll be more aware and intentional about not only what is currently happening in your life and business but also if those things are aligned with your overall visions. You may even discover that your big vision has shifted a bit and you need to alter your plans. If you're not reflecting and reassessing, you run the risk of spending copious amounts of time on something that isn't heart-centered, authentic, and building the future of your dreams. To put it more bluntly, you may be working really hard for something you don't even want.

If you don't take the time to *adequately* assess and reassess what you're working on, you'll be on a blind path to who knows where and someone else will be driving the bus. This is beyond goal setting. It starts with a big picture vision.

A lot of folks, perhaps even you, like the practice of goal setting. It feels productive. It gives you perspective and excitement— something to work towards. For many, goal setting is exciting because it feels like a "fresh start." It's a chance to tackle new things and, if you're doing it right, to really push yourself. But it's also stressful for some of us.

I used to fall into the "goal setting is stressful" category because it all felt too big, too difficult to achieve. I didn't know *how* to make these things happen. I didn't even know where to start. But I knew I had a good idea. A seed, if you will, of something that could be amazing. All great journeys start with one small idea and I was ready to start my journey. So I started small and began with vision. It started with something I call Dreamscaping.

Dreamscaping is the practice of sitting down and identifying what you want your life to look like. This approach fits work, career, and business into your dream life rather than the other way around. What will your dream life look and feel like? What will it allow you to do? Who do you want to be in your dreamscape world? How do you show up for yourself and others? A large part of this work is zeroing in on how you want to *feel* in your dreamscaped world—and how you *do not* want to feel. It is just as important to think about what you don't want as what you do want.

Personally I write out my Dreamscape in a journal or I use a voice memo app to speak it out loud and then transcribe. To my utter delight, different people have wildly different interpretations of how to Dreamscape. I'm not here to tell you how to do it or what it looks like because it's a personal experience and quite frankly, there's no *wrong* way to plan out your dreams! I will tell you what Dreamscape *isn't*. It isn't limited. It's your chance to think beyond your self-imposed limits, beyond what you imagine yourself capable of achieving, beyond what you think your ceiling is. Dreamscaping isn't meant to limit you, it's designed to unleash you.

Looking at Dreamscaping as a form of freedom was how Kristin, one of the IBE members featured in a previous Brave Spotlight, began a true transformation of her life and business. She wasn't convinced Dreamscaping would be impactful when I first suggested the idea to her. She thought the process was more like basic goal setting. It felt inauthentic and like a useless chore, one she'd done many times before. This time, however, I asked her to look at it from a fresh perspective. We approached it from the lens of The BRAVE Method and, for the first time ever, she thought about building her business around the life she wanted to lead rather than the other way around. This, finally, *felt* good!

Another client used to fight me on Dreamscaping. She felt like putting her dreams on paper was a commitment rather than a freeing exercise. She didn't want to be "tied down" by Dreamscaping. But when we started to dig into the endless possibilities and the ability to adapt and change her dreams and desires, she started to see new opportunities and was willing to give it a try.

In many cases, I ask clients to start with what they are certain they *don't want* when it comes to Dreamscaping. We may not always know what we want but we're, typically, pretty quick to say what we don't want. So reverse engineer it! Come at it from a unique and creative perspective. Turn it all on its head.

I have big dreams for myself, my business and my family. Many people would look at my dreams and think I'm overreaching or I've totally lost it. They may even think my dreams are unattainable. I don't spend much time worrying about what other people think. The BRAVE Method has taught me that what other people think is none of my business!

Nearly everything I've accomplished in my life has, at one time or another, felt unattainable. I dreamt of them anyway. I worked towards them anyway. Sometimes I find myself amazed at what I've created just by dreaming up impossible things and taking intentional action towards them. And when I think of all I'm visualizing and manifesting for my future, I get butterflies. Creating this abundant life of mine is filled with just the right amount of uncomfortable excitement.

For example, I know that at some point in my future I plan to live in Paris for at least six weeks of the year and have a second home in Puerto, Vallarta Mexico. Now I have no idea how or when these will become a reality. I'm not sure exactly how I will actualize these audacious dreams. But I know I will. Because I am a creator of unrealistic dreams. It's true I don't know exactly how I'll get there but by starting with this big, beautiful, bold dream I find myself *thinking* about how I might get there. What actions will I need to take? Who will I need to be in the process of making these dreams a reality? What choices will bring me closer? So each day when I visualize my future, I picture myself on the balcony of my Parisian apartment or my Mexican condo, overlooking the Eiffel Tower or the ocean, working, having team meetings and serving clients from wherever in the world I am.

Once I did some Dreamscaping and had an overall vision that felt really good, I created some achievable and immediate goals. I then broke those goals down into small, intentional, actionable steps. With only one little step ahead of me I got to work.

It's important to be able to see the big picture but you don't want to focus on the big picture all the time because it is way too overwhelming. Chances are you'll completely shut down if you look too far ahead at all times. I use something I've coined the "Vision to Action" formula to help me focus on the smaller steps. The formula allows me to get into motion and *stay* in motion. You can access the formula in the downloadable workbook mentioned at the end of the book.

When it comes to making reassessment a regular part of your life and business, try creating systems that naturally lend themselves to this type of introspective work on a daily, weekly, monthly, and quarterly basis. For most people this is a completely new approach. When I taught this approach to Kristin, the member IBE I mentioned above, she admitted she'd never set annual goals for her business! It turned out she was just functioning in the thick of the moment, without forethought or intention. While extremely successful, her business had been running her, rather than her running it! This new approach felt a bit revolutionary. In creating these goals she had a much clearer picture for how she would make her overall vision a reality. Annual goals are *not* the same as overall vision!

Let's consider a new approach to making your dreams a reality. Remember that attempting to goal-set before you properly identify your vision, and without a healthy dose of reflection and reassessment, isn't going to get you far. Just because setting goals allows you to feel like you've accomplished something doesn't mean you have. You may be spinning your wheels rather than gaining traction.

Think of it like going on an expensive, overseas vacation with some reservations and a list of great restaurants but forgetting to buy a plane ticket or having the cash flow to pay for everything. You simply won't get too far and the resources that you did have will be wasted! The trip *sounds* great, but it won't actually happen until you have all of the details and logistics in place. The same goes for goal setting. How in the world are you supposed to get where you're going *if you don't know where it is?!*

One of the reasons we struggle to actualize goals set at the beginning of the year is because we don't take intentional time to look at the past year and really assess and reassess what happened and how we want to move forward.

Remember I said reassessment should happen daily, weekly, monthly, quarterly and annually. So let's start with the big picture and work our way into the nitty-gritty, daily details.

Annual Reassessment

Annual reassessment doesn't have to happen in January. In fact, plenty of organizations have their fiscal year set to a completely different calendar. Decide for yourself when in the year you tend to feel the most inspired and excited to think big picture and make a goal for the year ahead. And reassessment isn't just for business! Doing this for your personal life can be completely game changing.

Your annual goals should fit into your overall vision for your life and business. They are the different buckets that must get filled in order for your vision to become and stay a reality. But remember, these annual goals are *not* your vision. They are the stepping stones to actualizing the vision.

Once you've identified your annual goal or goals (yes, you can have more than one) you'll want to make sure there's a viable path to victory for each goal. Now is when you map out the steps required to reach the goal(s) and remember these goals are steps to achieving the vision - everything builds off of the thing before it!

Create your annual plan based on the goals set and identify the sub goals required to make it all work out. This is where the Vision to Action formula comes into play. I suggest laying it out like this:

- Overall vision

- Macro steps (goals) required to achieve your vision

- Micro steps (small, actionable tasks) required to achieve the macro steps

- Pick the smallest, easiest item on the micro steps list and get into action.

Quarterly Reassessment

Now that you've identified your overarching vision and the goals that will help you get there, it's time to create some benchmarks for measuring success, ensuring you're taking the right actions to get to your destination and checking in with yourself, your team, your clients, your loved ones, and your dreams!

If you want something to actually happen, put it in your calendar. Give it a specific time and space for existence. Otherwise you're likely to put it off over and over again until it's an overwhelming task or no longer relevant. So when you do that annual goal setting and planning, get your calendar out and pre-schedule time for quarterly review and reassessment. If you need to include other people on your team or family in these meetings, be sure to clearly communicate when these conversations take place. This should not be a surprise meeting. It should be a standard, planned, and intentional part of leading a successful, brave life. This includes having regularly scheduled family meetings.

When doing your quarterly review ask these questions:

- What have we been doing?

- Are those things getting us closer to our annual goals and overall vision?

- What's working well? What isn't working well?

- What lessons have we learned and how can we implement them?

- What should we stop doing, do more of, do less of, or start doing?

- What are we celebrating?

Monthly Reassessment

Monthly check-ins and reassessments are a perfect opportunity to ensure things are on the right course and strategizing for short term sprints. This is the time to figure out where you can push yourself and the team just a little bit harder and strive to grow in new ways. Again, these should be pre-scheduled and anticipated by all involved. Make it even easier by scheduling them for the same day and time each month. For example, the 3rd Monday of each month at 10:00 am.

When doing monthly review and reassessment ask these questions:

- Are we on track to meet our quarterly goals?

- What went well this month?

- What lessons did we learn and how do we utilize them?

- What do we want to add into the fold that will help us get closer to our annual goals?

- What should we stop doing, do more of, do less of, or start doing?

Weekly Reassessment

This is where we get into what folks normally think of when they talk about "goal planning." But I'm flipping it on its head a little bit. This *is* goal setting but from the lens of reassessment. I recommend weekly reassessment happen before you close up your computer on Friday afternoon. Think about the week that just passed, check in with how you *feel* about the week. We achieve a healthy work-life harmony when we're honest about how things feel on a regular and consistent basis. Don't save this for the quarterly or annual reassessments! Stay on top of it! Again, these weekly commitments work best on the same day and time each week for consistency and planning. Don't push this to the side, prioritize the dedicated time! Schedule around it—make it one of your boundaries!

When doing weekly review, reassessment, and planning ask yourself these questions:

- How do you feel about the week that just passed?

- Did you show up as the best version of yourself?

- Did you follow through with your commitments? What about everyone else on your team/family?

- What got accomplished this week?

- What didn't get accomplished that needs to be a priority for next week? Or perhaps come off your list altogether?

- What does next week's schedule look like?

- Celebrate the wins!

Daily Reassessment

Having daily, intentional commitments is the key to being successful. These are the small baby steps required to put everything into play. Without these daily commitments you will *never* achieve your goals or vision. Ever. That sounds harsh, but it's just the truth. Without action, you will not make progress.

Author and friend Aaron Anastasi always tells me, "How we do anything is how we do everything."[2] And while some people find that controversial, if you really stop to think about it...it's true! Are you the type of person who buckles down and gets shit done or do you get easily distracted and things take you 10x the amount they should because you can't focus or push through? This isn't a value statement or a judgement. It's not that one way is right and the other wrong. We all process things differently. What makes you most successful is discovering what works best for you and planning accordingly.

Do you work best under pressure? Are you a procrastinator? I feel you! I've *always* put things off to the last minute. Even while writing this book I waited until as close to my deadline as possible to get the first draft together. I used to say it was because I'm a procrastinator. But several years ago while having a conversation with Aaron he threw out a pretty wild idea. "What," he said, "if you simply admit to doing your best work at the last minute? What if instead of using words that make you feel like a failure or cause emotional harm, you changed the story? Can you allow this new story to be true, and then schedule accordingly?"

It felt like a radical idea. Who in their right mind schedules things to be done at the last minute? And do we *really* get to allow putting things off to the last minute to be okay!? But then I spent some time really thinking about the possibilities. I asked myself "what happens when I put deadlines on the calendar that I *know* are far out from their due date?" I was radically honest with myself and admitted I typically don't do them. I push them off and allow more urgent (or seemingly urgent) fires to take their place. But the other thing that happens is that I carry a heavier load. I *feel* bad, I feel less than, I feel like I'm screwing up and I never show up for myself. None of these things are actually true.

So then I imagined what it might be like to say "I do my best work at the last minute" and schedule appropriately. I knew I'd get the work done because I had a deadline. Because I follow through and keep my commitments. I also knew that I wouldn't have weeks of sleepless or anxious nights that left me feeling like I was forgetting something or letting things slip. So I decided to give it a try.

And guess what? It worked! It still works. Sometimes the things we consider our weaknesses can lead to our successes. I no longer waste time putting things off and feeling shitty about it. I schedule the work to get done when it needs to be done and then I stay focused and dedicate myself to it. I do this through time-blocking (we will talk a lot more about this in the Action section of this book). My team and I use Slack (a team management and communication tool) to keep track of who's supposed to be doing what. It's a great self accountability system for daily commitments and reassessment. I also use a little app that I *love* called CommitTo3! I use the app to provide little, micro stretch goals for each day or to remember things that might otherwise slip my mind but I know will make a big difference towards the success of the day.

Whatever systems you want to utilize, build something that will help you make daily commitments and then follow through with them. Be sure to include time to truly think about the day ahead and what you want from it. I even keep commitments on the weekends for family, personal, or self-care related tasks! Ensuring you take intentional time for yourself and your family is absolutely crucial to one's success.

When doing your daily reassessment and planning ask these questions:

- Did I follow through on my commitments?

- What did I learn today that will impact tomorrow?

- Am I on track for achieving my weekly goals?

- Who can I ask for help or support?

- What am I grateful for today and who can I share gratitude with?

And remember, not everything you do will feel like BIG action. More often than not it will feel like insignificant action. But I promise you each and every little step you take will add up until you look back and realize you've created something amazing.

The seemingly small details are what makes everything work. The decisions and choices you make day in and day out to run your life and business are what will make or break you. Be honest with yourself in this process. What actual tasks have you undertaken? Are these tasks worth your time and attention? Are they helping you grow and reach a new level of success? Can you build upon them for your next phase of growth?

Without reassessment on a daily, weekly, monthly, quarterly and annual basis you'll, almost certainly, be leaving something on the table or hiding from some unfounded fear. Remember to practice radical self-trust. In order to do that you must be willing to look at the good, the bad, and the ugly in order to see the potential and the beautiful.

Brave Action

Dreamscaping

What do you want in the coming year? How about the next five years or ten? How do you want to get it and why does it matter? If you want to create realistic and achievable goals for yourself, get into brave action and start with dreamscaping.

Imagine your ideal life. Every element is exactly the way you want it to be. This is an exercise in thinking big but including all of the little details.

- Describe you...
  - dream life
  - dream job
  - perfect day

- How will you feel when you experience your dream life, dream job, dream day? Write it out with passion and zest

- Now describe how you don't feel when you experience your dream life, dream job, dream day

- How do you feel after completing this exercise?

Once you've done this you'll be able to more clearly visualize what you want for yourself. You can now begin to build these dreams because you have a clear picture for where you want to go. It's time to create the road map.

LIZ

BravE Spotlight

✳ Undoing History

Liz was one of the first people to ever join my Intentionally Brave
Entrepreneurs program. She was introduced to me by a friend
in the podcasting industry who came from the same ultra conservative community Liz was part of. As you may have guessed, I
don't often appeal to folks in ultra conservative groups. I'm a loud
mouth, outspoken, cursing, divorced lesbian! Trust me, I thought
the same thing at first. In fact I'd talked myself right out of coaching Liz before we even started because I thought "She will never like me. I'm too far off the beaten path for her." But, as it turned
out, Liz was looking to get off the path. She was tired of playing a
game she didn't design and following rules that didn't resonate as
truth to her. She was tired of being judged, misguided, mistreat-
ed, and held back. And she was tired of hating herself for wanting
these changes.

To truly understand Liz, you have to know that she had been
pushing boundaries for a majority of her life, and paying the price
for it. But, in the end, she decided that the legacy she wanted to
leave behind for her children was one of truth, strength, and willingness to question and create.

She started by building her own business even though the voice
in her head said "You have no business starting a business!" She
had no clear vision on where she wanted the business to go, or
how to get there, but Liz wanted to be a contributor to her family
while also being present for her special-needs child. She also wanted to have value and worth outside of being a wife, mother, and

homemaker. It was, finally, time to trust herself enough to see what would happen if she stood in possibility.

Liz's financial goals were not grand when we first met. She simply wanted to bring in enough income to cover the mortgage and help them get a little savings underway. And although, on the surface, this looked like it was about money, it wasn't about money at all. It was about undoing a lifetime of feeling small and misplaced. It was about finally deciding she was worth believing in.

Joining IBE took a serious leap of faith. It was a big financial investment for her, and perhaps more importantly, it was an outrageous commitment to make to herself. She had never given so much time, effort or money into her own health and happiness. I assured her that if she stuck with it, showed up, trusted herself and the program, and did the hard work, it would pay off.

And she jumped in, unsure, and pretty scared, yet willing. I watched her, day after day, week after week, show up, make new things happen, sign new clients, create new services and yet she never felt like she was getting anywhere. Then, one day, I asked her when she'd last gone through her business finances. Did she even know how much money she was earning? Turns out, she hadn't been including finances in her regular reassessment and reflection practices. To her surprise (but not mine) when she sat down and ran the numbers, she was earning more than her original goal had been.

Something about seeing these numbers unleashed a new phase of empowerment for Liz. Her confidence began to soar and she put herself out there even more. Business started growing and now she is looking at scaling and possibly even building a team of her own! Far more importantly though, she's learning to love, trust, and value herself. Her voice now carries and creates impact—simply because she believes that it does. None of this would have happened if she hadn't taken the time to reassess and see what's actually happening in her business. This stuff works, friends.

When we avoid looking at the details, the numbers, the experiments, the failures, the successes, it's because we're afraid of the answers. We don't want to discover it's "worse than we thought it might be" or we're afraid to disappoint ourselves. But if you never look at these things you also cannot see how far you've come or how successful you are, and you can't plan for the next phase of growth because you don't realize the first phase has been unlocked!

These enormous levels of growth don't happen overnight and they are not a quick fix. They take time and dedication. Pausing to really look at our growth and progress, rather than being afraid of what we might find, simply amplifies your growth opportunities. And if, when you review and reassess, you discover you're not growing in the ways you want, you can enact change and pivot. You truly have all the power here, if you're willing to give it to yourself! *

BRAVE Action

Set Up Reassessment Systems

Create your thoughtful and intentional reassessment and planning sessions by setting time aside to reflect and adjust accordingly. Take a moment right now to schedule time in your calendar for reflection of the past year. Seriously, stop reading and go do this.

First, consider the following when you do so:

- What worked really well?
- What didn't work at all?
- What did you most enjoy?
- What made you unhappy?

Then, be sure to look at the past year from every angle including:

- What worked financially?
- What worked for clients?
- What worked for your schedule?
- What worked for your loved ones?
- What was easy (or hard) to sell or promote?

Lastly, after you spend intentional time thinking about the past year in all of these different and meaningful ways, you can begin to cull and sort them.

- What do you want to do again?
- What do you never want to do again?
- What new things are you inspired to try?

It's time to goal plan! Now that you've looked at the past year and decided what worked and what didn't, you are ready to make some plans for the next phase. Set aside specific and intentional time for reassessment and planning on a daily, weekly, monthly, quarterly and annual level. Identify the dates and times for these sessions. Put them in the calendar and be sure to include everyone who needs to be at the table with you when these reflections and strategic planning sessions take place.

RACHEL

Brave Spotlight

✴ I Can Do That

Rachel is an educator. She was a teacher for many years and then moved into coaching and supporting other educators. And she's a completely free spirit. I've heard Rachel say she "doesn't like to be tied down" many times! She's also multi-passionate and felt that her job didn't allow enough space to spread her wings properly. There simply wasn't a variety of creative options in her job and she wasn't making the impact she truly desired.

When I first met Rachel our kids were in kindergarten together. Although I didn't know her well, she now tells me she "had her eye on me." While attending the school's annual fundraiser she spied the coaching package and gratitude journal I'd included in the silent auction.

Rachel is a woman who knows what she wants. And, prior to our first meeting, she'd decided she wanted to work with me because she *knew* there was something else out there for her, but she couldn't put her finger on it. It was time for a coach. But going into our initial conversation I wasn't aware of this. She was just a fellow mom at school who I'd never had a conversation with. But she walked in eager and ready, which was a treat and the beginning of a beautiful relationship that far exceeds that of coach and client.

It was apparent, in our first call, that Rachel had too many options in front of her. Narrowing down and focusing was proving challenging. She needed a little tough love and perspective setting. But what Rachel needed most was to sit down and reassess where she was, where she wanted to go and how she would get there. It turned out to be a winding road but on that first call she identified two important goals.

1. Be a full time entrepreneur within two years.
2. Create a conference focused on bringing play and creativity into our everyday lives.

I worked with Rachel in 1:1 coaching for six months. During that time she created and produced an incredible "Creativity Conference" that was wildly successful. She then, eagerly, joined Intentionally Brave Entrepreneurs to continue her growth trajectory and ensure that she and her business remained a top priority. By August, just a year and a half after that first call, she'd put in her notice and was running her own creative educational coaching business. Her client roster was stacked and her days were busy from the moment she went into full time entrepreneurship.

What she didn't think of doing for the first two or three months was to look at her finances. Money is scary for a lot of people. We don't want to look too closely, because what if we don't like what we see? But we played the "money on the table" game in our IBE cohort laser coaching session (which is an upcoming Brave Action) and she found herself curious. How much money did she want to be making each month and how close was she?

So she did the scary thing and looked back at payments received for the last few months and also what income was outstanding. Then she got really honest with herself about how far off that was from her monthly income goals. Turns out she was much closer than she expected to be! She would have totally missed that if she hadn't done financial reflection.

When Rachel told me about this experience I asked her how it made her *feel*. Her response was every coach's dream. "I felt like a total badass. Look how far I've come in such a short time! And now

I know I only need to sell a few more small products to meet my monthly income goals. I can do this!"

Armed with knowledge, motivation, and a game plan, Rachel identified what paths to take to make up any financial deficit and ended up knocking it out of the park. This is the power of reflection, radical honesty, and action taking. And it's a path that's just as valuable in our personal lives as our businesses. When we stop fearing money and learn that it's here for us, to support us, we open ourselves up to receiving in ways that may have seemed impossible before. ✳

Brave Action

Money on the Table

Oftentimes we plow through our work, head down and determined to just "get through it all." When we do that we risk missing some pretty important opportunities. That's why I love the "Money on the table" exercise.

This brave action requires you to be radically honest about where the gaps are in your life and business.

For business, ask yourself:

- What business is out there that I haven't followed up on?
- Who do I need to connect with to grow my referral network?
- What am I avoiding?

For personal, ask yourself:

- What opportunities are out there that I haven't followed up on?
- Who do I need to connect with to grow my network and opportunities?
- What am I avoiding?

And then take the following actions:

- Create a list of 5-10 people you would like to have in your referral network and reach out to them

- Connect with past clients in genuine curiosity to reconnect with them and offer support (you never know who will say yes!)

- Follow up on any unfinished conversations or contracts that are floating in the ether

- Identify 1-3 ways to bring income in rapidly (sit with this until some options present themselves to you!)

Reframing

"The antidote to anxiety is anticipation, where we choose to rehearse a result we actually want. Say it out loud. Write it down. Imagine what it will look like and feel like when you get it."

- Aaron Anastasi

I spoke earlier about limiting voices. These are powerful voices that are designed to keep you down, play it safe and not rock the boat. These voices aren't telling you the truth and they are causing a lot of harm. In this chapter I speak more directly to the importance of the words you chose to use, because *words matter.*

I like to invoke the Law of Attraction here: that which you put out into the world is what comes back to you. Think about that for just a moment. The words, energy and thoughts you give life to come alive. Thoughts become things and, in this way, we're able to create our own reality. Good or bad.

Many of us are so used to thinking negative thoughts and feeling badly that we don't know how to behave otherwise. Think about it for a moment: how does your body physically react when you start thinking negative thoughts? You get crankier, your body tenses up, your heart begins to beat faster, you have a hotter temper—all of these cause a negative effect on you and on the other people in your life—because we can't help but bring our energy into the room with us.

Positive Psychology teaches us that our minds cannot hold negative and positive thoughts at the same time. It isn't that we should never have a negative thought. It's what you do with those thoughts once they appear. There *are* going to be plenty of times you feel angry, sad, hurt, frustrated or any number of negative feelings. When they stick around, you give away your power. Making decisions when you're engulfed in negative energy is a dangerous place to be. How about flipping the negative on its head? Look for the positive in a situation. Find the silver lining or the crack in the foundation that will allow you to build something else. The universe always gives us what we need. Sometimes, however, we have to really look to figure out what the gift is. We often don't understand what's "for us" in a painful situation and that causes a lot of frustration. If you take a few steps back and start to think about the possibilities, you may be surprised by what you find.

This is where reframing comes into play. Rather than saying, "I don't know how to set up a new website." Try saying, "I don't know how to do that yet. But I know others who do. Let me ask for some support." See! It already feels better and more empowering. You are not stuck unless you want to be.

Or consider a more personal situation. Last summer we experienced unprecedented rains that left us and most of our neighbors with flooded basements. We're lucky because our basement doesn't flood often whereas our neighbors across the street flood nearly every time it rains. But during one particular storm, we feared water might be pouring in and, sure enough it was. We sprang into action raising boxes up and getting things off the ground. We thought about attempting to stop the water flow but it was a hopeless situation. Instead, after some reassessment and reevaluation, we chose to wait it out and not waste our time and energy on something that simply wouldn't solve the problem. We borrowed a wet vac from a neighbor and waited until the rain stopped. Once the water levels were no longer rising, we went down to the basement and got to work pumping the water out and cleaning up. Eventually, even our pipes helped by sucking the water back down.

If we had tried to stop the flow of water while it was pouring in, without reassessing and taking stock of the situation in front of us, we would have spent hours working on a project that we literally could not complete. It would've been futile in every possible way and that would have been frustrating as fuck! The downward spiral goes on from there. Defeated. Broken. Angry. Sad. Unmotivated. There are plenty of times where things are beyond our control but when we pause, look objectively, and then make informed decisions with the knowledge we have available, we can at the very least control our own energy and emotions through a challenging process.

When we start to think of challenges as opportunities and mistakes as lessons we're much more gentle and patient with ourselves. In turn, we're much more approachable, patient, and kind with our loved ones, clients, community members, and coworkers.

"Once your mindset changes, everything on the outside will change along with it."

- Steve Maraboli

By now you already know that mindset is important. The question is, how hard do you work on having a positive mindset? Do you have a daily ritual for staying in a positive place?

Our perception creates our reality. If you change your perception you have the power to change the future. So how do we go about creating that shift in perception? It starts with paying attention to your thoughts and words. There it is again...awareness! What types of conversations do you have with yourself? How do you talk about yourself to others? The words we use develop our mindset. Our mindset creates our reality. Therefore, if we use positive forces we develop a positive mindset and perspective. If you use negative forces, that's what you live with.

Your life's experiences give rise to a really distorted view of the world, a view that is observed through your self-made filters. There are stories that have shaped our lives. Stories created and shaped by parents, friends, partners, bosses, even the media. We have, over the years, begun to believe we *are* those stories. We convince ourselves that it's "just the way things are." When we start to question why we react and interact in specific ways, and how to alter those reactions, we begin to open the doors to writing new stories.

Let's work on identifying your position of power in any situation. I am going to say that again—YOUR POSITION OF POWER IN ANY SITUATION! There is *always* something you can do to shift a situation, at least a tiny bit. Even if the only thing that shifts is how you *think and feel* about a situation you have gained power over it. This all starts with altering the way you look at and think about things.

You have heard the old saying "the only thing you can control is yourself." This is 100% the truth and why it's so important to take a step back and assess. Identify what you can do to be in control of any situation as it relates to you specifically. Is it asking a question? Saying yes to something? Saying no to something? Making a phone call? Sending an email? Having a hard conversation? Walking away and releasing?

Asking questions, communicating well, and setting boundaries means everyone involved knows what to expect. Knowledge is power.

For example, while you may not be able to know when a client is going to return a contract you can sure as hell have a solid "closing statement" in a meeting, call, or email that gives you a position of power. Some examples are "When will you be making this decision?" or "Is it ok if I follow up with you next Tuesday?" or "When can I expect a response from you?"

This approach goes both ways—you're also in a position of power when you inform others of your expectations—"I will have this proposal to you by next Friday" or telling a family member that there is a specific day and time set aside to do something special with them. Having information puts people at ease. Whether you're the one getting the information or the one giving it—knowledge gives you power.

I want you to take this opportunity to move into a positive mindset by knowing that with just a little forethought and follow through, you can always have an element of power. Really begin to take note of thoughts as they enter your mind. Are they raising you up or making you feel heavy? If they're not lifting you, take the opportunity to turn them around. Literally: stop, assess the situation, and put intention towards reframing the thought in a positive manner.

Sales is always a great example for this type of thing. If you're an entrepreneur who built a new course and now it's time to sell it, you'll likely find several disturbing and painful limiting voices lurking about. Those voices may tell you all sorts of bullshit stories about why you can't *actually* sell the course, support clients, and make a lot of money. If you approach selling from that perspective you've already decided your product isn't worth buying, and that's the energy you'll bring into the process. Instead of thinking "If I can ever sell this course it will really help people!" Turn that around into "I have built this amazing course and I'm excited for those that take it to see a major shift in their lives." Focus on the end result and the outcomes, the rest will fall into place. Doing this takes awareness and practice. The intention behind your thoughts gives you power and creates a reality of strength, growth, and success. If you don't believe in yourself, no one else will.

TOM

Brave Spotlight

✳ Still Brave

One of the most impactful examples of capitalizing on your strengths I've ever encountered is a man named Tattoo Tom Mitchell. Tattoo Tom got his name because he is, literally, covered in tattoos all over his body. By the looks of him, Tom is an intimidating guy, to say the least. But it only takes a short conversation with him to realize he has a heart the size of Texas. After Tom lost his oldest daughter, Shayla, to childhood cancer, he dedicated his entire life to helping children with cancer and their families. He also works tirelessly to eradicate childhood cancer all together.

When Tom's 16 year-old daughter was first diagnosed he promised that he would fight cancer for as long as she fought it. That he wouldn't stop until she beat cancer. "She didn't win her battle against cancer," Tom told me when I interviewed him for *The Brave Files* podcast, "so I will never stop fighting."

This promise led to Stillbrave, the foundation Tom started in Shayla's memory.

Stillbrave is committed to helping the families of children battling cancer in any way they can. While children and their families are fighting the toughest war of their lives, Stillbrave will fight their lesser battles, so they don't have to. Stillbrave not only supports children with cancer, they help ease the burden of the family and the caregivers who are fighting battles of their own. Easing someone else's burden is brave.

Suffice it to say, Tom is a beloved "honorary family member" for each family he helps through Stillbrave. He sits in hospital rooms, plays dress up, brings parties, throws concerts and creates joy for these children and their loved ones day in and day out. Tom's heart and willingness to give whatever it takes to ease the pain and burden of the Stillbrave families is completely in line with leading from our strengths. He creates joy and leads from love. He's radically and unapologetically authentic. And while, upon first glance, you may find him rough around the edges, he is gentle, thoughtful, and remarkably kind. Tom can be trusted to protect and speak the truth. He is no-nonsense and takes no shit but if you will fight childhood cancer with him, he will be your ride or die. *

Brave Action

Reframing

This is a great time to start paying attention to the negative thoughts and energy that surround you. When you think negative thoughts, as we all do, write them down. Think about how these thoughts make you feel and then think about how you could flip the thought on it's head and use it in a way that will inspire, encourage or motivate you - or at the very least not make you feel terrible. Thoughts become things and awareness is a powerful tool in creating change.

- How would you describe yourself to others?

- Does this description match the way you think of yourself? If not, what is different? How would you feel if someone else described you the way you are thinking of yourself?

- Imagine it is a year from now. What does your life look like? What about your business? Write out, in great detail, everything you want to happen in the next year as if it has already happened. Leave nothing out. It's crucial that this be written in the past tense, as if you have already achieved all of your dreams in the past year so that you can begin living *into* this way of being.

- List 5 negative thoughts and provide turn-arounds to shift the thought into the positive. These turn-arounds should be the exact opposite of the negative thought—stick to this *even if you do not believe the turn around*! E.g. "No one will read my book" becomes "the right people will read my book."

- Look at your list of turn-arounds and identify at least one example of them being true. This is you intentionally disproving the negative thoughts! Gather your own evidence!

- Identify 3-5 situations where you can take action (even something really small) to put yourself in a position of power.

Resilience

We all have setbacks and they're bound to knock us on our ass now and again. The key is acknowledging the pain, discomfort, or loss; allowing yourself to feel it and understand it; and then, choosing not to stay down for long. Resilience is getting back on your feet with new information and a new plan.

You're already resilient. The honest truth is that you've survived every single day of your life so far. Even the unbearable days, the heartache, and any hardships or trauma you've experienced. Those things don't define you but your ability to get to the next day, that *is* part of what defines you. You. Are. Resilient.

But here's the most important thing to know about being resilient after a hardship, big or small: We almost never get back up on our own. As humans, we're not designed to go through life alone. It's not natural and it's not healthy. Asking for help gives us hope and support—two things we need most when we're recovering from a disappointment.

Resilience is an area that many believe we're either born with or we're not. But that's not true! Famed research scientist and grit and resilience expert, Angela Duckworth, has made the study of grit her life's work. When she was growing up, she wasn't considered smart enough and therefore her parents thought she wouldn't be successful, or at least not successful enough, by their terms. But she *is* super successful and she set about figuring out why in her revolutionary research. Angela has determined that her success is because she has grit.

Talent alone does not make a person successful. One can be the most skilled person ever, but if they don't apply themselves or learn from their mistakes and try again, they will, undoubtedly, *not* be successful. Angela shares that the resiliency it takes to be successful is something that can be taught. (I highly encourage you to read her book *Grit: The Power and Passion of Perseverance*.)

Learning to be more resilient has to be accompanied by a willingness to try and fail. Resiliency is derived from enough lived experience to know that making a mistake doesn't, in fact, kill us. In truth, those mistakes make us stronger.

Per Duckworth's research, resilience is made up of five pillars: self-awareness, mindfulness, self-care, positive relationships, and purpose.

When we work to strengthen these pillars, we foster resilience. And as such, when stressful things happen, rather than going into a downward spiral, feeling let down, or wanting to quit, these pillars work together to give us clarity, to calm the chaos in our minds, and give us a sense of control over what may, otherwise, feel out of our control.

RESILIENCE

| Self-awareness | Mindfulness | Self-care | Positive Relationships | Purpose |

Self-awareness

Self-awareness is about truly understanding who you are, including your strengths and weaknesses, your value system, what motivates you, how you process information and stress, and being honest about your feelings in any given situation. This deep level of awareness leads to understanding others better as well as how you perceive others' actions and how you will react in any given situation.

Mindfulness

Mindfulness is being actively open, aware, and involved in the present moment. By being mindful, you're able to assess your own thoughts and feelings from a distance without attaching judgement to them. They become simple facts rather than things that are "good" or "bad." Mindfulness also allows you to truly enjoy the moment you're in rather than living in the past or future. When you practice mindfulness you live into the idea of "be here, now" (which I happen to have tattooed on my inner left wrist). and that's a powerful gift to give yourself and those around you.

Self-care

Self-care refers to our ability, as humans, to function effectively and efficiently in the world while still maintaining a semblance of joy and happiness. It allows us to navigate the many challenges of daily life with a renewed sense of confidence, connection, and energy. Not a passive thing, self-care requires our active engagement, and—much like success, boundaries, balance, and bravery—self-care needs to be self defined. What does self-care mean to you?

Positive relationships

We are not a species designed to be alone. This is why we, often, end up surrounded by those that are unhealthy for us. Having a community of people who love and support you and for whom you want to offer love and support, leads to a significantly happier and more connected life. Recognizing that you're not alone and that others are in your corner gives us all more courage to step out as our most authentic and vulnerable selves.

Purpose

Purpose is the deep understanding that we're working towards something bigger than ourselves. Knowing your purpose helps shape your mindset and attitude towards others, what you're working towards, and how you experience all of the elements of your life.

Much of what you experience when you follow The BRAVE Method ties back to these five pillars of resilience. With intention and desire, you can strengthen all of these elements and, as such, your own resilience. Developing and maintaining these resiliency skills take a lot of intention, hard work, and practice. Resiliency won't happen by accident. You must choose it.

It's worth nothing that resilience is *not* about pushing through on things that you have no love or passion for. Angela Duckworth says, "If you're really, really tenacious and dogged about a goal that's not meaningful to you, and it's not interesting to you - then that's just drudgery."[4] No one wants that.

Growing Grit

Grit is passion and perseverance for long-term goals. Angela Duckworth's 2013 TED Talk is all about finding the key to success and through her research with Martin Seligman (the father of Positive Psychology) she has proven that grit is a key indicator in someone's ability to be truly successful. Through her extensive research she concluded that success is not about IQ, talent, family income, or other factors. The most significant predictor of success is, in fact, grit.[5] She concludes that it's about working long and hard in pursuit of a higher purpose. It's about fostering the growth mindset and rising after supposed failure. And it's about following through even when it's difficult to do so.

Contrary to what most of us grew up believing, success really has little to do with talent or skill. Yes, in some cases, like acting or professional sports, you need talent or skill to even be considered but those that truly achieve in these areas are the ones who put in the most effort. According to Duckworth, talent needs to be combined with effort in order for it to turn into skill. And skill needs to be combined with even more effort in order for it to become an achievement.

There are two ways to grow grit, according to Angela Duckworth.

1. Inside out.
2. Outside in.

Growing Grit from the Inside Out

Growing grit from the inside out requires you to focus on four specific areas—Interest, Practice, Purpose, and Hope. Duckworth uses the word "Interest" rather than passion because it feels like a more achievable and common concept for people to grasp. By doing the work of discovery, development, and deepening of your interests you'll better understand yourself and your passions.

Intentional and deliberate practice, according to Duckworth, includes setting a clearly defined stretch goal, being "all in" by giving your full concentration and effort, asking for feedback to improve weaknesses, making it a habit through repetition, reworking it and refining when things don't go right, and not trying to do it alone!

Interest and Practice are about you. They are internal motivations. But Purpose is about others. It's the intention to be part of the solution and to contribute to the well-being of others. This is where you think about what problem you're solving and how solving it helps the greater good.

Finally, Hope. Hope is the belief that it will all work out in the end. It's understanding that while the road may be bumpy, you can achieve your goals, make a difference and get where you want to go. Hope is about knowing that failures and challenges are not permanent and you can rise above them.

Growing Grit from the Outside In

We're all stronger when we work together. My partner often quotes her mother in saying, "Many hands make light work." And while sometimes that saying annoys the hell out of me because chores suck and I don't want to do them, she's right.

In fact, we have this wonderful Christmas tradition that was passed down from my mom. Each year my kids pick out their own special ornament for the Christmas tree. The premise being that when my kids move out and have their own Christmas trees they will have a collection of ornaments to get started and a boatload of happy childhood memories to relish. As you can imagine, that's a lot of ornaments on our tree with all these kids! We also collect ornaments from our travels and special events. Each year we pull out all the ornaments and decorate the tree together. It gets done faster, my kids feel some ownership in decorating the tree and it's also a very special time for us to reminisce on each ornament, and where we got it from. This always creates a true sense of belonging and being part of a treasured family unit. It makes us laugh, and sometimes feel sentimental. It's, inevitably, everyone's favorite part of holiday decorating.

Working together and doing the hard thing teaches us follow through and discipline. It leads to new levels of growth and learning. But sometimes so does a trip down memory lane, to see how far we've come. Growing grit from the outside in is about learning what makes you, or your work, unique and how you, as an individual, make a difference for others.

We grow grit from the outside in when we create or participate in environments that value discipline, provide support, and encourage learning. All of these things are action oriented. Some are self -guided actions, others are impacted by the people we surround ourselves with. Each of these elements are important when learning to be more "gritty." But the one thing they all have in common is that they all require some type of action!

ANOUSHÉ

Brave Spotlight

✳ Breaking the Mold

Anoushé Husain is one of the most inspiring, incredible people I've ever encountered. Born missing her right arm below the elbow, Anoushé's constantly breaking the mold and challenging her own potential – both physically and mentally. Even as a cancer survivor who also battles multiple, life-long chronic illnesses, she lives boldly with a brave outlook on life.

With the constant love and support of her parents, Anoushé was always encouraged not to let her disability get in the way. She was introduced to competitive sports as a child and began to thrive. Unfortunately, as a teenager she started to experience excruciating pain in her joints that forced her to quit competitive sports.

Eventually she was diagnosed with a rare disorder called Ehlers-Danlos syndrome (EDS), a disease that weakens ligaments and tendons in your body causing overly flexible and frequently disconnected joints. When she quit competitive sports her Ehlers-Danlos got much worse. She was in constant pain and discomfort.

Because her parents had never raised her to feel broken or flawed, and due to the mental skills she gained growing up with sports, Anoushé simply wasn't the type of person to just lay down and give up on life. When a friend suggested she attempt rock climbing, however, she literally laughed out loud. It was hard to get from the bedroom to the kitchen. How in the world did her friend think she was going to climb a rock wall? This would be a diffi-cult task for someone with two arms. And it's worth mentioning that Anoushé is Muslim and wears a traditional Hijab. So, yeah, imagine climbing a rock wall with only one fully functioning arm, severe chronic pain, and a Hijab.

After some coaxing and encouragement Anoushé decided to give rock climbing a try. Turns out, this was a motion her body would let her do. Being active again breathed even more life into this inspiring young woman. It was her sheer determination that led her to discover the healing power climbing provides. For Anoushé these moments allow her to fully escape the challenges of normal life—it's a time to be free.

Knowing the importance of bringing sports to differently abled people eventually led Anoushé to starting a social initiative, Paraclimbing London. The organization, as a whole, aims to make climbing more accessible to those with physical, mental, or emotional disabilities. Climbing sessions are completely free of charge and cater to each individual's needs. Paraclimbing London focuses on inclusivity in a fun, empowering way and provides an escape for those facing all sorts of challenges in their daily lives.

When I spoke with Anoushé on *The Brave Files* podcast she shared that sometimes cooking (which she loves to do) is hard. Taking showers causes excruciating pain and can only be done a few times a week. But being a competitive climber gives her the mental and emotional strength needed to make the rest of her life work. She's still in constant pain, but she has the mental prowess to push through the hard stuff to get to the part she loves and needs to thrive. And she does it through sheer grit and determination. ✷

BRAVE Action

Finding Your Resilience

I've had numerous clients tell me they just aren't as resilient as me. Whenever this happens I simply pause and remind them that they are here, in this moment, showing up for themselves and not allowing themselves to quit. That's some powerful resilience, if you ask me.

In this BRAVE ACTION I want you to find your own resilience.

How do you react when things don't go well? Do you shut it all down and walk away for good? Do you allow yourself some time to be frustrated, angry, or sad and then make a new plan? Do you blow right past it and pretend it never happened?

Which of these responses do you believe is the most resilient? The answer is the middle one. The most resilient thing you can do, when things go wrong, is allow yourself some time to sit with what happened. Feel your feelings and experience the natural flow of things—and then make a new plan and get back to work. Make time to grow your own resilience.

DALE

Brave Spotlight

* Embrace the Fear

One of my favorite things is when people eagerly introduce me to their brave friends. I consider it such an honor when others see something in me that reminds them of someone they know who's braved the odds and come out winning. That's how I met Dale Spencer.

When Dale was twenty years old, he made a split-second decision that left him paralyzed from the waist down. His first inclination was to throw in the towel but with the love and support of his family, friends, and college professors, Dale learned how to be resilient and thrive despite knowing his life would be forever altered.

A mutual friend introduced me to Dale via email. He was eager to meet in person and we set up a time to connect at a local coffee shop. In an unusual stroke of luck, I was early to this meeting. I tend to run late for, well, just about everything! But on this day, I was early and I'm so glad I was because I got to see Dale pull into his parking spot and get himself out of the car, into his wheelchair, and make his way into the coffee shop. He literally rolled right in like it was the easiest thing ever. Then, once we'd had proper introductions, he proudly showed me a video of himself downhill skiing—a life long dream that he'd recently made come true. You can find the video on the podcast website under the show notes for Dale's episode "Embrace the Fear." I promise you, it's worth watching!

When I started *The Brave Files* podcast I knew I wanted to interview Dale. He was one of the bravest people I'd ever met. Not just because he managed to live a full bodied life without the use of his legs, but because of the way in which he lived his life—full of zest, passion, power, and compassion.

As public speaker and trainer, Dale helps folks embrace their fears. He was one of the first fear fighters I ever teamed up with. Our mutual goal is to help people truly understand that their fears were holding them back and that, if you let them, seemingly tragic experiences can often lead to surprisingly wonderful results.

Dale's life is also a reminder that we're not alone. He didn't re-build his life by himself. None of us do! No matter what you're go-ing through, there are others out there who have been where you are and can help you. Resilience, it turns out, is easier to build with a strong support network around you. Likewise there are people who will come up behind you that need to see you step into your brave and be resilient. Your brave actions may serve as a beacon of light for others on their own journey.

Resilience is a skill that can be taught. I'm willing to bet you're a hell of a lot more resilient than you think you are. Look at all you've survived and accomplished so far in your life. You keep showing up and there's really nothing more resilient than that. ✳

Leaning on Your Strengths

I'm going to let you in on a little secret: it's okay to do the things that you're naturally good at instead of pushing yourself to "get better" in areas that aren't your strengths. Don't get me wrong, I want you to get uncomfortable! I want you to stretch yourself but this can be done within the realm of what you're naturally good at and not by torturing yourself with that which is extremely challenging for you. I do believe that *everything you really want is just on the other side of uncomfortable*. But I also believe that the most important step in starting something new is to just start. And it's easier to start if you're utilizing your natural talents and strengths. Stop letting your fear and limiting voices prevent you from trying the next new thing. Once you start, you can then layer in levels of complication to increasingly push yourself past your comfort zone.

I have a note taped on my desk that says, "You don't have to be great to start, but you have to start to be great." I truly believe in starting by any means necessary. That often looks like breaking things down, making them easier and more achievable. It's ok to go for the low hanging fruit! Many times, in order to start, you need to begin with something you're already good at.

Take, for example, a program I created several years ago, Chaos to Clarity. It's an online, self-guided audio course and building it was, admittedly, drudgery. My original plan was to make it a video-based course. But despite all my best efforts, I could *not* get traction with building the course. It was like a heavy weight was on me and wouldn't allow me to get to work.

When I was really honest with myself, however, and took the time to reassess and reflect on what was happening I, finally, figured out what my block was. Video. Ahhhh, that's what was tripping me up! People love video and everyone says it needs to be included—but for whatever reason video and I don't get along. And I was avoiding building the course because I wanted to avoid video.

This is crazy, right? I have a theatre degree and am completely comfortable on stage and speaking in public. I network and connect with people all the time. I lead workshops with ease—but when you put me in front of a video camera, without a live audience, things go whacky. Now, several years later, I have a slightly better relationship with video but it's still a struggle to push myself in this area unless I have people to engage with.

The moment of breakthrough came while chatting with a friend who was staying with us for about six weeks. My friend, Sunni, was a nomad for a couple of years and would trade her skills and services for housing. This was her second stay with us and this time we traded for a strategy session, which was her speciality. I started talking about the course and sharing my struggles in creating it. And to my surprise, Sunni casually said, "Why does it have to be video? Why not make it an audio course?" Wait. What!? How had I convinced myself that video was the only option here? I was absolutely not thinking creatively and outside of the box. Granted, this was before I started *The Brave Files* podcast so I wasn't an expert at audio either but it was far more aligned with my natural strengths and comfort.

The idea of an audio course instantly appealed to me because I've always loved audio as a form of learning and media consumption. I love being able to listen on the go. Whether I am in the car, making dinner, on the couch or in the shower, I can consume media and still go about my daily business. Video, on the other hand, tends to annoy me, even as a consumer.

And as it turned out, I had recording equipment on hand because my then coach had gifted it to me as a gentle nudge towards starting my new podcast. Everything was right there in front of me. I had what I needed to succeed. All I had to do was embrace a new perspective, actually show up for myself, and do the work. Embracing something I was already good at, and comfortable with, allowed me to work through my block. It gave me the freedom to get started on something that had the potential to be great. I may have eventually gotten there on my own but that one conversation with Sunni is what helped me open my eyes to possibility. Being open-minded to conversations and ideas from others is a true gift when you want to do things you've never done before. I love a collaborative approach to problem solving!

Taking my Chaos to Clarity course from video to audio is what, eventually, gave me the knowledge and confidence to create *The Brave Files* podcast. You just never know what will take you to the next big idea! So while I *do* want you to embrace your inner bravery, to push through and find things on the other side of your comfort zone, I don't want you to use "it's too uncomfortable" as an excuse for being stagnant. That excuse is bullshit and you deserve more from yourself.

BRave Action

Character Strengths

Through my study of Positive Psychology I learned about the extreme importance of our natural abilities and character strengths. The old school approach to "success" was to strengthen your weaknesses and get "better" at things you're not naturally good at. The good news is that business as usual isn't business as usual anymore and this backwards approach is on it's way out. This concept is turned on its head when we learn that science tells us we're better off leaning into our strengths rather than trying to improve our weaknesses.

This is a remarkable discovery, actually. In the early 2000's, scientists discovered 24 character strengths that make up a common language and this language indicates what is "best" about each of our personalities. Each and every one of us possess all 24 character strengths in some capacity. However, we all have a unique character strengths profile.

The 24 character strengths are categorized under six broad virtues. These virtues are universal across cultures and nations and all people, regardless of race, religion, location, social or economic status, gender (or anything else) possess these virtues.

Those six virtues are:

- Wisdom
- Courage
- Humanity
- Justice
- Temperance
- Transcendence

One of the things I found most fascinating in studying these six virtues and character strengths is that we are far better served to learn from, lean into and utilize our top five character strengths rather than trying to "improve" those at the bottom of our lists.

This is because when we are good at something that comes naturally to us, we thrive. Imagine what we could do if we chose to see and appreciate our own strengths and the strengths of others rather than focusing on our own, or another's, weaknesses.

Sure, you can reassess your strengths and weaknesses, but actually *knowing and choosing* to play to your strengths *is* choosing to grow via grit and resilience. You have everything you need. Nothing is missing from you, working with your strengths gives you the upper hand. It provides proof that you are creative and resilient. Essentially it creates the conditions for you to genuinely flourish.

When we take the time to intentionally develop awareness of our top strengths it allows us to focus on what's strong rather than what's wrong. The VIA Character Strengths[6] website says;

> "Leveraging the science of positive psychology, we now can identify the strengths that define who we are at our best—the qualities that, when nurtured, can improve all areas of our lives. Character strengths are those aspects of our personality that define what is best in us. Collectively, they are responsible for our greatest achievements and fulfillment. Scientists have identified twenty four strengths that are the basic building blocks defining our individuality, psychologically speaking. We each possess all twenty four of these strengths in different degrees and combinations. These strengths are universally valued—in the East and in the West—across the world's diverse cultures. Positive psychologists define them as positive traits that are beneficial to self and others. They lead us to positive emotions and relationships, greater vitality, and meaningful life activities. We flourish when we identify and flex our strengths.

The key is developing an awareness of our strengths and how to optimally use them, in order to boost our resilience and well-being. If we're conscious of our own strengths, we're more likely to recognize strengths in others, leading to more harmonious relationships which are especially needed during these challenging times. Once we know what our best qualities are, they open up a vital pathway to engagement—at work, at school, in relationships, and through the peaks and valleys of life. Due to the science of positive psychology which focuses on what's strong about a person, versus a problem-focused approach, people can learn to design their own future powered by their strong suits."[7]

To learn more about your character strengths I urge you to take The VIA Survey of Character Strengths (viacharacter.org). It's a free self-assessment that takes less than fifteen minutes. This assessment provides tremendous information to help you understand and utilize your strongest qualities. Access VIA Reports to receive a personalized, in-depth analysis of your results, including actionable tips to apply your strengths for greater well-being. I, personally, retake this test every six months because our core strengths shift and change as we do!

I also want you to make a list of the things that you're really great at and find ways to infuse those talents and skills into something that you've been putting off. What can you shift or change just a little by taking something that you're afraid of and approaching it with a skill that you have already mastered?

Bonus "R"—Reset!

See, I told you I was always adding to The BRAVE Method. This R didn't even come to me until I started writing this book! It's important to always remain open to change and growth. Change is, after all, the only constant. I find when I practice what I preach, The BRAVE Method constantly moves and shifts with my life. It provides everything I need to grow, be flexible and creative in my endeavor to live a big, bold, brave, beautiful life. In those moments of change I have to remind myself that even though I may feel stuck I'm not. We're never stuck unless we decide to be and it is never too late to change—sometimes it just takes a pause and a reset.

Focus Your Energy

Sit and reflect on the areas of your life and business that need your attention most. Identify if it's your business or personal life that needs the most attention and improvement. Then, focus your energy in that direction.

Ask yourself a few questions to ensure you're staying in alignment with your values and overall goals:

- Did any areas of your life or business suffer during off or unusual months (like summer, unexpected personal experiences, or the holidays)?

- How can you direct your energy towards those areas?

- What habits can you implement today to set you on the right track? Or which habits would you like to change?

- What are you most excited to improve upon right now?

Refocus On Your Goals

Keeping these answers in mind, begin to think about your goals. Are they still the same as they were a few months ago? Our dreams, desires, and priorities shift regularly; don't miss an opportunity to stay in touch with yourself on these things! If your goals have shifted, this is the perfect time to really dive deep and reset.

It's important to evaluate the specific, daily changes you'll want to make in order to achieve this newly identified priority. Break your big goals down into smaller, actionable tasks. Reconnect with your "why." All of these things are crucial when it comes to refocusing on your goals.

Now Is The Time

When it comes to staying in alignment with your goals, *now is always the time to start.* When you wait for the perfect time, you'll quickly realize there simply isn't one. Join me in committing to finish strong—whatever it is you start. Ditch the things that no longer serve you because "being busy" isn't something to celebrate. Let's focus our energy and make things happen!

Action and Accountability

Nothing Works Unless You Do

Nothing works unless you do. "A" is all about getting into action. It's not in the thinking of things where change and growth occur, it's in the doing of things!

You can have the smartest, most brilliant ideas in the world but if you never do anything with them they are just ideas. Someone once accused me of being a "do-ist" and encouraging a "do-ist culture with my coaching." They spewed it at me with so much hatred and anger and I couldn't help but laugh. Why yes, I thought. That is exactly what I am. I am a DO-IST!

I have never been one to tolerate listening to people complain about stuff but not be willing to do anything to change it. It, truly, makes me insane. Why anyone would choose to sit in their own shit constantly is something I'll never understand.

But I've learned that it's more complicated than that. Due to limiting voices, past experiences (even past trauma), and mental health, some folks simply cannot see any way out of the nasty mental and emotional situations they are in. Some people spend their entire lives living in a dark hole of unhappiness. It's one of the saddest things I have ever seen. I've learned to be more patient and accepting of it, even if I don't actually understand it.

I spent a great deal of time in my own hole of darkness and unhappiness. Staying in a marriage that didn't work or make me happy, hiding my truth from myself and the world. I felt so small and so incapable of changing the narrative. At the time I couldn't identify what was making me so unhappy. But once I recognized that my misery and fear-based life were a result of being untrue to myself, who I was and wanted to be, and how I wanted to live my life, I started to see glimmers of light. I stayed in that hole for a really long time. But I also dug my way out of it. I don't win any special prize for this—people do it every day and it doesn't make me special—but I know it can be done and knowing is half the battle.

Change is inevitable. So you're either going to be building a life that you don't love *or* you can choose to build one that you do love. You actually have all the power here, if you're willing to use it. When what you've always allowed to be acceptable is no longer acceptable you *will* create the change you desire. Once you're aware of the desire to change, it's on you to actually *do* something about it. Don't get me wrong, none of this is easy. The concepts are very simple but they are in no way easy. They are, however, really really worth it. Everyone deserves to take a deep breath and build a life they love. Even you.

Typically by the time folks find their way to me they have seen enough light to think that, maybe, possibly, it doesn't have to be "this" way anymore. All you need is a glimmer of hope, a tiny seed to plant in order to grow something magical.

Thinking there may be a way out is the first step to creating real, intentional change, but you can't stop there. When a client walks into a meeting with me and they present all of their issues, limiting voices, tolerances, and bullshit holding them back I coach them through creating manageable, sustainable change. Creating change is about taking action. And the bitch of the situation is that *no one can do it for you.* You can have the best coaches and mentors on the planet, you can spend thousands of dollars and get the best advice in the world, but none of it matters if you don't show up and do the fucking work.

Choosing to take action and do the work doesn't mean your heartaches aren't valid or that your past experiences have not harmed you. Accepting that these things are facts you can't change is accepting what you can't control. Identifying new ways to grow through—and despite—the discomfort is controlling what you can. The BRAVE Method is about changing what you can control and changing your mindset about the rest.

This is why ACTION is so very important. If nothing ever changes, nothing ever changes.

Sometimes Taking a Break Is the Right Action

Every once in a while it gets a little quiet on my social media platforms, my online groups, and my blog. When this happens, my instinct is to say "sorry!" But truthfully, I'm not sorry. Sometimes I find myself knee-deep in new projects or working with clients and my focus needs to shift. Sometimes the amazing members of Team BRAVE get sick or take a vacation, and something has to give. On top of these normal work things, I'm still a mom of four and have a partner that deserves my attention. Sometimes I just need a fucking break and I've learned to listen to that inner need and lean into it.

There are always going to be times where we feel a little over-whelmed, under-appreciated, and just plain exhausted. I especially find myself feeling this way during the holidays, or during winter in general. And like I said, when the going gets tough, something's got to give!

During the pandemic I even started implementing regular, quarterly, solo-retreats. I book an airbnb someplace a few hours away from home and go off the grid for 5 days. During these retreats I rest, walk, spend quality time planning and visualizing what I want for myself, my family, and my company. I read a lot and cook for myself. Most importantly, I focus solely on myself and fill my own buckets with love, attention and joy. And prioritizing myself in this way has had a tremendously positive impact on my life in every way possible.

I've learned it's extremely important for me to have alone time! Learning to get good with myself, trust myself, love myself, show up for myself, and get really honest, without distractions. Being alone can be scary for some folks to think about, but there's so much we can learn about ourselves when we spend time alone. You don't have to take extended solo retreats like I do! Even if it's only an hour here and there, find time to prioritize yourself without having to give or take energy from someone else.

It's more than okay to take a break sometimes. In fact, it's necessary for a healthy, brave life. Taking a break allows you to focus, wholly, on yourself or something else that may pop up and take unexpected priority. I've learned to build in breaks and to allow them to be action items in my life! For example, I always take my daughter's birthdays off to spend the day with them. I do this for my partner and my own birthdays also. These things are important to me. They're a serious form of self-care and they make me better. I am a better coach, teacher, and parent when I take time out and do things for myself and my family. These are lessons I hope each of you will take firmly in hand and implement on a regular basis. Take care of yourself. Set some things aside – and do it unapologetically. They will be there when you are ready to come back.

Brave Action

Grit—Asking for Help

It's time to have a truth-telling session with your-self right now. Imagine you're 90 years old and you're in exactly the same place you are right now, at this moment.

- How do you feel?
- What do you wish you'd done differently?
- What would you never change?

Grow grit for new levels of success.

- List out your interests and how you pursue them.
- How often do you practice the things you want to become better at?
- What is the higher purpose of your interests and passions?
- What do you hope for?
- Who are the people that can support you in learning, growing, and doing hard things?
- How often do you connect with these people?
- What do you want from these relationships? Are they providing what you need?

Delegate, Delegate, Delegate

One of the bravest things we can do is ask for help. What was once thought of as showing weakness is now a clear indicator of success. When you embrace the fact that you don't have to do it alone or that others' skills and expertise might help you achieve even more than you would on your own, you're growing your business and growing yourself.

My own coach once told me that the best use of his time was to be coaching or making efforts to get into conversation with people he could potentially coach. For him, that meant delegating and outsourcing other aspects of his business which pulled him away from being in conversation with and serving others. He also admitted he simply was not good at and didn't enjoy some of the more traditional business roles like marketing and administrative work. Truth be told, I'm in the same boat. While I'm competent at marketing, social media, bookkeeping, and administrative work, it's not my strong suit and, as such, takes me much longer than it would someone with more skills in those areas. Having my coach as a role model in this way, to see him as perfectly imperfect was freeing and inspiring to me. It showed me a path I'd not previously considered before.

When I first started out as an entrepreneur I tried, *hard*, to do it all on my own. I didn't think I had the business, income, or right to have any support at all. I also learned quickly that I didn't know all the answers or have all the skills required to be successful as a one-woman show. This was a dangerous position to be in. It left me stuck and playing on a small field. Plus, it was a lonely place to exist.

The reality is we simply cannot do all of the things on our own and we shouldn't have to. We're not good at all things and if we are being honest, we simply do not enjoy all things. Yes, there are some things that must get done when you own your own business, but that does not mean you need to be the person actually doing them. Give yourself permission to build a team and begin delegating. If this is something you already do I encourage you to find new ways to delegate. Trim the fat and streamline those processes as much as possible. It might mean giving up some control but there is a lot of freedom in that once you get past the fear of letting go.

Recognizing that you can't do it all is key. Figure out what you do really well and then do that thing. Delegate the rest to someone else. Do you know what I'm really good at? I'm really good at being a coach. I'm really good at giving motivational talks and facilitating workshops and learning experiences. I am really good at planning events. I'm also really good at knowing who else is really good at their job. So, I put people in positions to do their magic. Allowing experts to play an active role on my team makes me look good. They are smart! They elevate me. They help me level up. I trust them, and they trust me. We work together collaboratively as a team.

It's also important to keep in mind that building a team can look a lot of different ways! You can build a team at home with childcare, someone that comes in to help you clean once a month, subscribing to a meal delivery program, or simply asking your family members to take on more of the load.

From a business perspective, you have the ability to build a powerhouse team right now. Trust me you do! Even if that's a person who comes in for two hours a week to clean up email, schedule social media, or write a blog post. When you start to look at all of the different ways you can delegate and grow you'll quickly see all of the opportunities in front of you. It's truly like getting more hours in the day! And don't discount the power of the trade and barter system, especially when you're first getting started. I've traded babysitting with friends so we each get some time to ourselves and I've traded coaching for numerous other, business-related tasks to help me take things off the ground. This isn't something I'm required to do anymore but I wouldn't be where I am today if I hadn't done those trades. The barter system is alive and well, my friend! There are a lot of ways to have a client and a lot of ways to get paid! It's time to think out of the box. That's what making the brave leap is all about. Fuck the rules. Fuck the ceilings you've placed on yourself. Fuck what society says. Fuck the way it's "always been done." This is your life. Do it the way you want and get creative about it!

Bottom line, it's best to spend your time doing the things that only you can do. That's how you will be happiest and successful (and make the most money). If it doesn't require your brain, make a brave leap and get support. You'll earn way more profit, in the end, if you get yourself out of the minutiae of the day-to-day stuff.

JASON

Brave Spotlight

* Asking for Support Isn't a Weakness, It's a Sign of Strength.

I don't just work with entrepreneurs. I also do a lot of executive coaching for corporations and organizations. One of my clients, Jason, was referred to me by a partner in his firm. I'd been supporting, coaching, and creating with the partner that referred me for several years and I know when she suggests someone work with me it's because she sees serious potential in them. She wants to give them a hand up and an edge as they work towards promotion and, eventually, partnership in their firm.

When Jason first came to me, he was a highly productive workhorse. He was one of the most dedicated members of the team and could be counted on for just about anything. But the problem was, Jason didn't know how to go from being a doer to a creator. He didn't know how to relinquish control or trust the team. And he totally sucked at delegating responsibilities or asking for help. He also had a confidence issue. As is often the case, Jason's lack of confidence presented itself as being cocky, which he isn't. The real culprit was a deep seeded fear of looking weak.

But Jason, much like Molly whom I mentioned in a previous chapter, knew what he wanted. He wanted to become a partner at his firm. He wanted to be a kind, thoughtful, passionate, and dedicated leader who was respected and admired. Some of these things, like kindness, thoughtfulness, and passion, were natural skills for Jason that he hadn't yet fully recognized. He simply had to learn how to amplify them and use them to enhance his leadership abilities. And he quickly realized that respect and admiration would be natural byproducts of intentional, thoughtful, and inclusive leadership fueled by kindness and clear communication.

Jason went all in with coaching. He took everything we worked on to heart and he showed up, over and over again no matter how uncomfortable or challenging the work was. He was 100% committed to doing and trying anything I suggested because he knew it would enable him to grow in ways he wasn't able to do on his own.

Jason tucked his pride in his pocket and showed up willing to try and explore new things that were so far out of his comfort zone that I'd often laugh before suggesting a new approach. But each and every time he just said "Ok. I'll give it a try." And he did!

So Jason learned the power of growing grit from the outside by delegating to outside sources and allowing me and others to coach and mentor him. He surrounded himself with people he admired and trusted and was willing to try new things even if others gave him a hard time or didn't see the benefits right away.

He was so good at trying new things, in fact, that other folks I coached at the firm would call or email and say "I can see the Heather in Jason right now! It's working!" We recently had a catch up conversation and he said something I will never forget—"I hear you in my head all the time. When I'm getting frustrated or angry I think 'what would Heather do' and I do that thing." This totally makes me laugh by the way. I like the idea of being the voice in my client's heads if it helps them take the action they need to. It just goes to show you never really know the impact you'll have on someone else's life. I wonder who's hearing *your* voice in their head right now? Is it a positive voice? One that inspires growth and change?

Months after I stopped working with Jason he emailed to tell me he'd won an award at his company. He was being recognized for his efforts and strengths as a leader and he felt that a lot of his growth was due to working with me. Having clients come back and share their positive experiences is something I am forever grateful for and humbled by.

It's also worth mentioning that Jason didn't just get into action working on himself. He also learned to delegate, to ask for and provide feedback, and, perhaps most importantly, to trust his team and himself. He learned that to lead a team of strong, successful leaders you have to relinquish some control and allow the people you've put in place to do their best job. Relinquishing that control wasn't a sign of weakness. It was a strength.

Most of us are not raised thinking "many hands make light work." Instead we're told to put our heads down, and get our shit done. We're taught that asking for help means we aren't capable of doing it ourselves and we're *supposed* to be able to do it ourselves. That's utter bullshit, by the way. Women are expected to carry the burden without showing the strain, men are expected to have all the answers and never show signs of weakness. Bullshit. Bullshit. Bullshit. This is why we stay in small, unsatisfying and unhappy lives. Believing this load of crap is dangerous and it's time to toss it all out the fucking window.

So many people believe asking for help is for other people. You may even encourage others to ask for help but be uncomfortable and unwilling to do so yourself, even when you know it would be appreciated. Here's the hard, honest truth—When we ask for help, we give others the opportunity to support us, which most people are eager to do. Getting others involved provides ownership and buy in. When others believe they have a voice at the table and you trust them, they begin to show up more empowered. This means your delegating and getting support might be just the thing to build a stronger, more impactful relationship.

Jason did this and he created schedules, time blocking, boundaries and so many other things that combined are one powerful force for making the brave leap to delegate more. The leap is still scary but it gives you a whole hell of a lot more confidence when you jump!

This is just further proof that you don't even have to believe me when I say The BRAVE Method works. Jason didn't believe me at first either. In fact, he couldn't imagine how these things would create the change he desired. But he had committed to going all in and trying everything. And guess what, it worked. Because The BRAVE Method *works*!

If you're ready to create the life of your dreams, feel good in your own skin, and make an impact on the world, all you have to do is get started and give it a try. The proof will appear before your eyes once you do. ✳

Brave Action

Deciding What to Delegate

Sometimes goals are big; sometimes they require an intense amount of planning. Of course, some are small and easy to dissect. However, if you have big goals, break them down into small, manageable steps. This is how you find success!

Start by listing your big picture vision, then identify the goals that will help you realize that vision. From there list out all of the small tasks required to achieve each individual goal. You know you can't do it all, or at least you can't do it all well—how do you decide what to delegate?

Start by creating a few lists:

- What tasks must get done to keep your business (or life) running properly?

- What personal skills do you bring to the table?

- Which of the tasks in the above list do you actually like doing?

- What tasks could easily be delegated?

- What tasks simply cannot be delegated?

Then begin delegating!

- Identify who could do the work required.

- Research virtual assistants, contract workers and other professionals who could meet your needs. You can even consider working a trade or barter with other professionals if you both offer something the other desires.

- Have clear expectations and communication systems with those supporting you. Ambiguity leads to chaos.

- Get started!

Once you do these things, you'll suddenly have time to do the things you're most passionate about. It will create a sense of freedom and you'll be in a position to do your best work, live your best life and experience far more abundance in the process.

Productivity and Effectiveness

This book is about throwing the notion that fear should hold you back straight out the window. It's about making the brave leap into the unknown because you know there's something great out there, you just have to find it!

I've talked about the importance of identifying your needs and defining and creating boundaries but now we need to kick it into high gear with new levels of productivity and effectiveness.

There have been several times in my life that things felt so out of control that all I could do was shut down and scroll through my Instagram feed. I thrive on routine and structure. With four kids I'm not sure I could function without it. Any time my schedule is thrown off my natural instinct is to go into shutdown mode, not overdrive. I think, "there's so much to do. I don't know where to start. I'm not going to do anything." What I've discovered is that having good efficiency systems in place goes a long way towards preventing breakdown. So instead of doing nothing, my system is to do small, manageable commitments and rebuild momentum. This strategy really came into play during the pandemic when I'd just launched my Intentionally Brave Entrepreneurs program. I had a lot of work to get done but all I really wanted to do was crawl back in bed and cry. I did cry a little, but mostly I just broke all my tasks down into even smaller tasks and did them one baby step at a time. I also ran coaching sessions and team meetings from my bed because there were always six or seven people working and learning remotely in my home. It was a madhouse! It was a time of imperfect action but it turned out to be exactly what everyone needed. Everyone I encountered or coached needed some grace and patience. It was a time to let go of societal standards and expectations and bring realness to the forefront.

Time spent in an unproductive manner just causes frustration and a backlog of work and responsibilities. I can't tell you the countless days I spent feeling so far in the weeds that I had no idea when I would ever get out. There is always so much work to do! During those times it was all I could do to get client needs met, never mind working *on* my business—I felt like I was drowning inside my work! This is no way to live and it certainly is no way to run a successful business.

Productivity is a buzzword in the entrepreneurial community but it makes all the difference in the number of hours spent working on and in your business. I actually want you to think of this more as "effectiveness." What tools and resources make you more *effective*?! You're not a damn computer!

How you spend your time is the deciding factor in how long it takes you to complete the tasks at hand. Are you super focused? Are you constantly squirreling from one thing to another, flitting around checking email, looking for social media notifications and answering phone calls? STOP THE MADNESS!

Tiny side note here…let's talk about the word NEED. I NEED to work more, I NEED to get more clients, I NEED to close this deal, I NEED to make dinner, The "I Needs" can go on and on, right? Remember the story I shared about my daughter. Do it because you want to and be honest about why you want it. That's the drive you're looking for!

Stop Multitasking right this instant!

It's time to face the truth. Multitasking is causing a whole lot more harm than good! Multitasking is a nasty thing that we are trained to praise. However, the truth is you can't do anything 100% if you're attempting to do other things at the same time. Quality work and meaningful connections simply aren't going to happen when you're zapped of energy and spread too thin. *How you spend your time matters.*

There's no way around it. We look at these people who are highly productive and wonder how they achieve all they do. You might even feel the sting of jealousy when you admire all they've accomplished. I mean, how in the world can she run a super successful high, six-figure business and still have time to connect with her family every night?

But I'll let you in on a little secret: Highly productive people create habits around the actions they want to take and they don't try to do everything on their own. There's nothing superhuman about it. They work hard to weave positive habits into every aspect of their day. They manage their time efficiently because they've made a habit out of doing so. Whether they depend on a detailed morning routine, block their time for important tasks, or something as simple as spending 30 minutes every single day marketing their business across social media channels, their habits are the key. Successful time management creates real balance and it leads to freedom!

Here are a few of my best systems for productivity and effectiveness.

- Create a morning ritual. It doesn't have to be meditation, simple self-reflection can do the trick. Even 5 minutes alone with a steaming cup of coffee counts.

- Do the things you need to do (but may not really want to do) first. I call this "eating the frog" and tell you more about later in the book.

- STOP multitasking and START batch tasking. This does not mean you cannot have multiple projects going on at once. It simply means you only focus on one thing at a time.

- Pick up the phone. Sometimes having a five minute phone call can get the answers that you or someone else needs right away without a day's worth of email back and forth.

- Schedule out your day. Trust me, just do it. In most cases, it doesn't matter what task is first but having a schedule to tell you where to begin means you are spending less time in overwhelm and chaos. Sometimes people think schedules tie them down, but they actually offer freedom. When you follow a schedule you get more time back in your day because you're not spending all of your time distracted or figuring out what to do next.

- Keep your to-do list to no more than 6 items (I actually prefer three, but up to six works).

- Utilize some of the many, amazing productivity apps and plugins available for your computer, phone, or tablet.

These are just a small sampling of tools to manage your time. Implement these systems or design your own—I promise that doing so will allow you to discover there are simply more hours in the day. You will also start to notice you're happier, loved ones are happier, and clients are happier. When you're focused, everyone gets the best of what you have to offer! Now that is totally badass.

MAXWELL

BRAVE Spotlight

* Flexibility and Adaptability

Maxwell Ivey is known as "The Blind Blogger." But Maxwell wasn't always blind. He began to lose his vision at age twelve and was fully blind by the time he was 22 years old. Blindness, however, wasn't ever an excuse for not doing everything he wanted. The son of carnival owners, Maxwell, had a fierce and intense drive towards all that still lay ahead for him.

Learning to navigate life without vision meant a lot of obvious changes for Maxwell. He shared with me on *The Brave Files* podcast that the greatest gift blindness gave him was the ability to stay flexible and adaptable.

It's easy to make excuses, Maxwell says. The real magic happens when you don't use those excuses and you make things happen instead. This focus on flexibility permeated every aspect of Maxwell's life. Not only did he physically adapt to new ways of moving through his day, but he also learned to stay flexible in his work. After exiting the carnival business, he created a website to sell surplus amusement equipment. Working in the online space is difficult for most, but it's a gigantic feat for someone who is blind! This work eventually led him to starting a blog, becoming known as The Blind Blogger, and producing an entire line of books and products called "What's your excuse?" and a podcast by the same name.

The core of Maxwell's advice lies in the notion that if you are willing to be open to the direction the universe is guiding you, if you're adaptable and flexible, you'll be on the right path. He also reminds us that there are always people out there willing to help and support you. You just need the courage to ask for it. They can't say yes unless you ask!

The things I most appreciate about Maxwell are his sense of humor, calm, and confidence. Because he spent so much of his life learning to go with the flow, be flexible, and try new things to get a desired result, Maxwell finds he's always successful, even when things don't go as planned. Success, much like bravery, must always be self-defined and there's an awful lot of freedom in that! ✳

Brave Action

Productivity and Effectiveness

- Identify at least three systems, processes and strategies you already have in place for personal life, household, and business.

- List out any needs you have that are not being met by your current systems.

- Research if any systems you currently use have the capability to do anything on the previous list.

- Come up with three new systems, processes and strategies to implement for personal life, household and business.

What steps will you put into plan to actualize and utilize these new systems, processes, and strategies?

Accountability

I've never been great at holding myself accountable for things I didn't really want to do. I'm probably not supposed to admit that to you but hey, this is a radically honest space, right? When my kids and partner aren't home, I often eat chips and cereal for dinner and I never make the bed. I'm known for leaving a pair of shoes on the floor for far too long and losing my airpods, requiring me to spend ages finding them.

I don't call my parents as much as I should (yuck, I just "shoulded" myself). This is actually one that makes me feel bad. Why do we not do things and then not doing them makes us sad or upset? I'm going to work on this one. Because I know we can't get the time back and this is one area I never want to have regrets in.

But I'm a systems girl. I love systems and the way they help me stay on task without having to think about them too often. I've spent a great deal of time creating systems that help me remember to do the things that are important and not disappoint myself or others. Ok, I still eat like a frat boy when I am home alone, but that's not often and I've decided to let it be ok. That's one of my favorite things about intention, choice, and empowerment, just like boundaries—I get to decide what's ok! I get to decide if I want to allow something to make me feel bad or not. If it does then I do something to change it and if it doesn't then I stop treating myself like shit over it.

If you're going to make the effort to make the brave leap, if you're working on identifying what you really want, creating boundaries, and getting into action, then it's crucial to add an element of accountability. If you don't, shit just won't work the way you want it to. Because we need accountability to stay at the top of our game. Hell, we need accountability just to stay *in* the game most of the time.

One of the systems that I've set up for myself are different accountability relationships. Now that I have TeamBRAVE, an entire team of people to support me with my many work commitments and goals, I'm accountable to them. I even have them set deadlines for me and put them in our shared knowledge system. I love living free and wild, but if you want something from me by a certain date, then you need to set a deadline for me and communicate it with me!

I do a fairly good job of staying accountable at home because I want my kids to learn to do so themselves. So the keys get hung in a certain spot (most of the time). The coats get hung up in the back (again, most of the time). The trash gets emptied (fine, my partner does this chore!) and the bathrooms cleaned. All on schedules so we all know what to expect and when. We're accountable to one another.

For years I was also a member of a mastermind group that met every other month. In these meetings we would talk about big picture business plans and then brainstorm different ways to make things successful. I loved this group because I was always so bogged down in the weeds and details of the "every day" but these meetings allowed me to think on a grander scale.

And then I was introduced by a wonderful client to a fellow podcaster, named Eddie, who, as it turned out, would completely change my life. Eddie hosts a podcast geared towards the wedding industry and my client thought I'd make a great guest for his show and that we should know each other in general. That was one of the greatest gifts anyone has ever given me and it was just a random "OH! You two should know each other" kind of moment.

Eddie and I hit it off right away. I was a guest on his podcast and then I invited him to be a guest speaker for my audio course, Chaos to Clarity. Eddie, who lives in New York City with his wife and kids, is the founder of a tech startup called Timeline Genius. They take the hard work out of creating wedding and event timelines and if you've ever created one of those timelines you know what a pain in the ass they are!

After Eddie and I recorded his section of Chaos to Clarity he said, "So, I have a kind of crazy idea. Are you interested in being accountability partners with me? We could talk once a week and just really push each other to get shit done and support one another."

Although this took me by surprise, I was intrigued and honored so I readily agreed. When the universe drops something magical in your lap, take it! We started off each week with a little check in and then we'd both admit our frogs for the week (this concept comes from Brian Tracey's book, *Eat That Frog*. The idea is that if you do the thing you least want to do first then everything else is a win!). We would challenge each other, push each other and support one another.

Eddie has been my accountability partner for many years now and we talk regularly. Sometimes these calls are deep thinking, existential conversations that completely blow my mind. Sometimes they're simply focused on the week ahead. But they're never fluffy. There's a depth to my conversations with Eddie that always leaves me with a feeling of support, encouragement and just a little more strength to power through. Despite both of our businesses growing tremendously over the last several years, this relationship continues to push us. It really doesn't matter where we are, we support each other in getting to the next level. We've seen the transformation before, we know what to expect, and we know we can see it in each other again and again. This accountability game never ends.

Last year Eddie discovered a little app called CommitTo3. He'd started doing it with his wife and they were both enjoying it. The idea was to record your top three commitments each day and then share those commitments with everyone on your team. I was invited to join the team that has since grown to five of us. We call ourselves Team Life Allstars—because we're showing up and doing the hard work to be Allstars at this thing called life (Prince reference 100% intended here). We partner this with a text thread where we cheer one another on, share motivational concepts and simply offer a lot of love and encouragement. And if I ever send a message that sounds like I'm struggling you better bet your ass I'll get a phone call from Eddie within a few minutes. "Ok Heather, what's going on right now? Let's talk it through. It's going to be ok." There's just no replacing an all-in, no holds bar, accountability partner.

Over the years our calls have shifted a little. They used to be focused on the details and the specific tasks ahead for each week. These days we spend more time talking about the big things in our hearts, minds, and businesses. We call each other on our bullshit pretty quickly and help think through options to overcome obstacles we're each facing. Everyone should have an Eddie in their life. A straight shooter and deep thinker who has your back in every way possible.

While accountability can sometimes be hard, it can also be multifaceted. Several years before meeting Eddie, I met a woman on Instagram and we bonded over the fact that we were great at sharing things we were bad at. We excelled at telling the world what our failures were but we weren't good at sharing what we were *actually* good at. So we, randomly, decided to create a "wins" accountability relationship. This was not your typical accountability relationship. For almost a year, we would have a quick chat on Friday mornings and share our wins for the week.

We both knew some ground rules were going to be important so we agreed not to do something that I see so many people do—"discredit the wins" before sharing them. You know what I mean, right? It often goes something like this, "Well, I didn't do everything on my list but at least I got some of it completed." Yuck. When we discredit ourselves before we even start we already feel bad. Why even bother sharing the good things because we're already a disappointment to ourselves and others? I hear it every day when I'm coaching and have had to make it a rule for all my clients to avoid discrediting themselves before they even share the win.

With our ground rules in mind, my new "wins" accountability partner and I agreed to simply state our wins and cheer each other on. That was, literally, the entire conversation. But what this relationship gave us was a reason to stop and appreciate our wins as they happened throughout the day. In order to have a list to share with one another, we were required to keep a running tally of our wins for the week. Thus allowing us both to pause regularly to recognize and acknowledge the amazing things happening all around us. It was an unexpected and welcome gift.

You aren't required to have a "wins accountability" partner to keep a list of your wins, but it's truly something special to declare what you've done well each week and have someone else give you a little extra love for it.

Creating Accountability

One of the most important things you can do to avoid feeling overwhelmingly alone is to have accountability systems set up. Here are a few great ways to use an accountability partner or partners:

- A specific accountability system, like mine listed above, where we share wins.

- Identifying weekly "stretch" goals (perhaps things that you would otherwise put off!) and then checking in on each other weekly.

- Developing Mastermind groups with three or more people to work through what is on your plate and come up with creative plans for achieving your goals.

Accountability is a key to achieving your goals and following through on your commitments. Another benefit of an accountability partner(s) is having someone by your side to help you stay motivated!

These partners can be friends, colleagues, or a professional coach and you can have more than one (I do!). No matter who it is, having someone by your side to help you stay on track is imperative. Knowing you're accountable to others and that someone else is behind you, cheering for you, is empowering.

Finding an accountability partner can seem daunting. Making friends as an adult is sometimes a challenging thing. However, it's always good to simply reach out to those in your field and people who seem to operate on the same level you do or maybe someone you admire and want to learn from. Whether you already have a relationship with this person or it's someone you meet via social media, finding an accountability partner you vibe with can have a profound effect on your life and business. I also have accountability partners that are not in my industry but are successful professionals that I admire and respect. When thinking about building accountability relationships remember not to limit yourself.

ANGELA AND MAUI

Brave Spotlight

✳ An Unlikely Pair

As part of the Intentionally Brave Entrepreneurs program, I spend several weeks getting to know each cohort member before I assign them to an accountability partnership. This is because the curated group of individuals come from a vast array of backgrounds and interests. And one of the reasons I assign rather than allow them to self assign is to push folks a little out of their comfort zone, allowing them to interact with someone they may not naturally be drawn to and to get a perspective that's incredibly different from their own. I've found it one of the most impactful components of the program and here's why.

These relationships are, almost always, successful and in many cases life-changing. Some stand out more than others and when I think about powerful accountability partnerships I always think of Angela and Maui. These two are about as different as possible in most ways from race, gender, sexual identity, chosen career, religion, and even overall personality and demeanor. But one thing I knew they had in common was their deep passion for kindness and humanity. I knew they would learn a lot from each other and I never doubted that they would be kind and compassionate towards one another.

To my joy, Angela and Maui jumped into their newly formed accountability partnership with both feet. They, almost instantly, started sharing little glances of knowing and understanding. Speaking truth to the other's power in our group sessions, celebrating and praising one another, but also calling each other out on their bullshit when necessary. It was obvious this relationship was thriving and it began to serve as inspiration and guidance for other IBE members.

Angela told me she was nervous to receive her accountability partner. She feared this person wouldn't be able to handle her larger-than-life personality, that they might try to handle her with kidgloves, and not be able to take constructive criticism from her direct approach. Angela, a sexologist and coach, put it like this, "I was afraid this new partnership would be more work for me and I didn't have time for that." She didn't want to be in "coach-mode" when it came to accountability.

Maui, by comparison, had no expectations of his accountability partner but he knew his tender soul needed someone who would be kind and loving in their approach. Perhaps from the outside, Angela didn't seem like the right candidate. She has this tough exterior. But because I knew that underneath the tough shell was someone with the softness and drive, she would be exactly what Maui needed. And so they were paired together.

Having a regularly scheduled accountability call has been a game-changer for Angela and Maui. They meet, virtually, every weekend and sometimes even have a virtual meal together. Maui says Angela is the organized one that helps keep them on schedule. They spend this time together focusing on honest conversation and deep listening. It's a time to hear what's happening in one another's hearts and lives, not just at work. And they use these calls to support in whatever way is most needed. They often say to one another, "What do you need from me today?" And the answer ranges from simply listening, to a little push, clear advice, or perhaps straight-up calling each other out.

Having an accountability partner that asks "what do you need from me" requires a lot of self-awareness and leads to empowerment. It forces you to know yourself, ask for what you need, and trust that someone else will hold you in this time and space rather than harm you. This is true ownership of yourself and your needs.

I actually interviewed Maui and Angela before writing this Brave Spotlight. I wanted to get their honest perspectives on their accountability partnership. During the interview, things came to a sudden hush, filled with emotion, when Angela shared that, for her, this is the best, easiest, and safest space to practice vulnerability. Maui truly knows her triggers and blocks. He knows when she's showing up authentically and he gently calls her out when she's not being true to herself.

Maui tends to shut down when things get hard. To retreat into himself. This past year has seen tremendous growth for him and his new company. He quit his day job and dove into his own business, which has taken off like wildfire. But it's also been filled with personal difficulties and challenges. He often feels extreme joy and excitement while simultaneously feeling sad and depressed. He shared that having Angela in his life to support him and check in has helped him avoid shutting down and retreating from the moments in his life. He has been able to remain fully present and to rest when that's what is called for but also to push past the fear and blocks whenever possible.

Neither Maui nor Angela could have anticipated the personal relationship that would bloom from a business coaching program. They feel like this is the sibling relationship they've both longed for.

With tears in her eyes, Angela said, "Maui fills a space in my life that I knew I needed but didn't believe could actually be filled."

When I asked them to share their best tips for having a healthy accountability relationship they said to approach the relationship from the perspective of being a helper and always asking what the other needs. Also, know your own communication style and be clear about that from the start so you're always on the same page.

Maui also said, "Make sure you trust your accountability partner enough to let down your guard and step into the space emotionally open. If you're closed off this won't work." He went on to say, "we often section off the more intimate parts of ourselves and reserve them for romantic partners or family members. It's rare to have that intensity and intimacy with others. When you realize these intense levels of intimacy and communication with someone who is a platonic friend, and allow yourself to reach that point, some pretty incredible things can happen." *

BRAVE Action

Creating Accountability

Ready to get started? Here are some action steps:

Think about the people you know, work with respect and feel a kinship with. Who among them might make a good accountability partner?

- Identify two or three people who can help you stay accountable.

- Reach out to them and gauge interest in creating an accountability partnership.

- Once these relationships are established, clearly lay out how you can help one another reach your goals.

- Schedule recurring check-in times, ideally the same time every week for consistency.

- Don't over commit. These check-ins don't have to be long; they can be as simple as a 5-15 minute phone conversation fit snugly in the middle of a busy day.

- Be a good listener to your accountability partner. Supporting them and helping them think through their needs will make you stronger.

Your Personal Board of Directors

You'd be amazed how often folks comment on my "super woman status" and that they don't know how I "do it all." This always makes me smile and laugh because *I don't do it all!* No one can do it all. If it appears someone does it all, I can promise you there's a team behind them making it look easy. I could never do it "all" without my people—my personal board of directors (PBOD).

That's right, my community, my people, my personal board of directors. My partner told me recently that I juggle all the balls better than anybody she's ever known, and I make it look easy. While that is a really fantastic compliment, I am here to tell you I could not do it alone and I'm often wondering how long I can keep up the act. Sometimes I want to let a ball drop because the weight of maintaining the juggling act is too much to bear. My PBOD is what helps me stay sane, on track, and feeling supported. Sometimes they take one of the balls so I can have a moment to catch my breath.

Your PBOD are people you choose to surround yourself with who will encourage you, tell you the truth, provide emotional support, challenge you, dream with you, hold you accountable to your goals, call you on your bullshit—*be your people.*

They're the ones you rely on to give authentic feedback, act as a sounding board, and advise you in the midst of life decisions, opportunities, and challenges. They see the bad. They celebrate the good. They love you through the ugly.

The best PBOD is one that's diverse and willing to provide you with multiple perspectives, ideas, and insights. What you don't want is an echo-chamber or a group of people who think exactly as you do or who will say what you want to hear.

That's why, ideally, your personal board of directors shouldn't consist of immediate family or partners, as they might be too personally invested in an outcome to provide guidance that is purely in your best interest. The success of your PBOD really depends on being surrounded by those that are cheering for you and are totally in your corner, but aren't emotionally invested in a personal way. That means they stay honest, analytical, and objective.

Are you wondering who's on my PBOD?

Well, my friends, the ones who drive my kids to birthday parties and bring them home from school when needed. The few special, lifetime friends who I may not see often or even talk to on a regular basis but, somehow, just when I need it, they reach out with a call or text simply to say "You're on my mind. You matter. I love you." These are the friends that I know would drop what they're doing and fly across the globe to save me if I really needed it! TeamBRAVE (the collection of incredible individuals who help make my business successful), one of my mentors, my accountability partner, my walking buddy—collectively they create a team that keeps me functioning at my highest level, because let's face it: I can't do it all.

Professionally, my PBOD are the people I go to when I need to flush out an idea or pursue some new, crazy thing that I've just come up with. The ones who say yes when I send an email and say, "Oh my God, can you help me think through this idea right now?"

I'm always acutely aware of my community and how much I depend on them but the best part of having these supportive people in my life is being able to give back, as much and as often, as I get. When the opportunity arises for me to show up and help my community, I do so joyously, graciously, and with enthusiasm. It's important to ask powerfully so you enable others to give graciously. I have certainly nailed down the "ask powerfully" part. I long ago gave up the notion that asking for help made me weak. Instead, I realized that asking for help actually gives me strength and a place of empowerment. It gives me the confidence to know that I can get it all done because I don't have to do it alone. Still, my favorite part is the "give graciously." My PBOD gives graciously over and over and over again, and I love the opportunity to pay it forward.

Brave Action

Create Your PBOD

It doesn't matter if you're a business owner or not. Having a Personal Board of Directors is impactful, empowering and worthwhile. Do you already have a personal board of directors? I'm willing to bet you do. Take a look at your close 1:1 relationships and consider what role they play in your life.

- Who do you talk to when work stress becomes too much?

- Is there a neutral person you lean on when you want to talk through relationship challenges?

- Who do you go to for solace when you can't pull yourself out of a bad patch alone?

- Who has been there for you through thick and thin, despite the years and distance and life that may have happened for each of you?

Think about the people that came to mind as you went through the list above. They just might be your PBOD and you didn't even know it! It's important to note that unlike a corporate board of directors, you're not gathering these folks in a room once a month and having a group go at your life. These are personal relationships that, combined, support you in all the ways. Essentially they are your personal support crew. Society doesn't often encourage us to focus on relationships outside of "best friend" or "soulmate." Yet these relationships can be as deeply fulfilling, beautiful, and definitely as important to your wellbeing as those of immediate family.

If you haven't already identified your own PBOD I suggest you get one immediately, right now, the second you finish reading this chapter! I promise you, it will change your life!

Vulnerability

This section on vulnerability is a companion piece to the "getting radical" chapters coming up next. It takes radical vulnerability to be a successful leader, business owner or contributing member of society. It means admitting faults, asking for help and not always having the answer.

When we're completely vulnerable we risk people thinking we're weak, lazy, or small. But the truth in vulnerability is actually the opposite of these things. Vulnerability requires us to release ourselves from shame and just work with what we've got.

If you will allow it, vulnerability can be a powerful tool in any emotionally intelligent leader's toolkit. One trait that all courageous leaders have in common is their willingness to leverage their mistakes and faults into genuine connection, creative problem-solving, and learning. These leaders embrace vulnerability in themselves and nurture it within their teams by acknowledging their current situations, taking responsibility for their emotions and actions and asking for help.

When a leader acknowledges that they don't know something, they begin to foster an environment of imperfection. While this may sound bad, it's actually quite good. "Perfectionist" environments are unhealthy and dangerous. They set up unrealistic and unattainable expectations that, eventually, lead to unhappy employees and disappointed clients. Perfectionist parents have the same effect on their children.

Several years ago I had an unexpected conversation with a past client, Palak. I'd worked with Palak for years helping her understand herself, gain confidence and, eventually, make Partner at her company. But one area that was still challenging for her was appearing as less than perfect or making mistakes. Culturally, failures were detrimental and owning them was terrifying. But that day, our conversation was about her daughter. Her perfectionist daughter who was, literally, torturing herself in an effort to be perfect. Sweet Palak was heartbroken and so very worried about her child. After she shared her story and concerns, I paused for a moment and said "Have you ever admitted making a mistake to her?"

"What?!" She yelped. "No! I would never want her to know I made a mistake."

"Well then," I said, "this is your problem. She is learning from you that it's not okay to make mistakes." When you allow yourself to be truly vulnerable and honest, you open up the floor for deeper connection and honesty for everyone in the room. It builds trust and elevates performance. It gives other's permission to be themselves, to make mistakes, to fall flat on their faces and know that it does not mean they are no longer of value. Being our most authentic, vulnerable selves allows those around us to do the same.

In her work researching shame and vulnerability, Brené Brown teaches us that while we all struggle with things, sharing these struggles is not a sign of weakness. It's actually an incredibly effective and powerful way to build trust. Thus, the art of vulnerability is about truly belonging to yourself and to others. Although I love all of Brené's work, her book *Braving The Wilderness* is my favorite. It calls to me like a favorite poem or love song.

Someone once asked me what book I would leave behind, if I was only allowed to leave one, for future generations. My answer is *Braving The Wilderness*. I urge you to read it, but I'll leave you with this. Vulnerability is about belonging.

> *"True belonging is the spiritual practice of believing in and belonging to yourself so deeply that you can share your most authentic self with the world and find sacredness in both being a part of something and standing alone in the wilderness. True belonging doesn't require you to change who you are; it requires you to be who you are."*
>
> **- Brené Brown,** *Braving The Wilderness*[8]

ARLAN

Brave Spotlight

✳ Creating a Seat at the Table

Arlan Hamilton is a well-known name in the venture capitalist world but she's not exactly a household name. That's why it was so strange for me to hear about her twice in one week from both my partner and my step-sister.

Having written her new book, *It's About Damn Time,* and on a promotional tour, Arlan did something pretty unusual and opened up her calendar to 30 podcasters for interviews. It was first come, first serve for these spots and each podcaster would get 20-30 minutes of Arlan's time. I didn't know who she was but my partner said "get that interview! It's a big deal." So I secured a spot and then got to work learning about this woman.

I quickly discovered that Arlan Hamilton's life experience and the trajectory of her career were nothing short of extraordinary. In less than five years, she went from experiencing homelessness and sleeping on the floor of the San Francisco airport, to being the only Black Lesbian to successfully build a venture capital (VC) firm, from the ground up.

For Arlan, it was about deciding she wanted a seat at the table. She got curious and vulnerable along the way. Although she had no idea how to break into the VC world, she knew this was her destined path. What she chose to do was start researching startups, Silicon Valley, and the venture capital space. This would allow her to "know what the investors know" when she started raising capital for her own business. Her research highlighted the startling fact that over 90% of capital is awarded to straight, white men.

In a study by American Express, Black women are starting new businesses at a rate of six times the national average, yet receive only a tiny fraction of VC funding. White men, on the other hand, constitute less than a third of the US population, but they capture nearly all VC funding.

Discovering this fundamental lack of fairness set Arlan on a path where she asked herself three important questions:

1. What would it look like if the person writing the checks was a Black, Gay woman from Texas?

2. Would the people getting checks start to look different?

3. And, would that change things for the better?

The past five years of Arlan's life are proof positive that the answer to these questions is yes, yes, and HELL YES! Her company, Backstage Capital, has funded more than 130 companies in the past four-and-a-half years and averages approximately 20-30 per year. Backstage Capital focuses exclusively on funding companies led by people of color, women, or LGBTQ. In an amazing twist of fate, Arlan regularly receives attention from celebrities, politicians, and powerful VC players. This has forever changed the landscape of who and how companies get funded.

This story of the first Black, lesbian, woman venture capitalist is brought to you by extraordinary vulnerability. Arlan share's her own story of heartbreak and brokenness to help lift others up from their low places. She believes in and invests in others in ways that no one was willing to do for her. This act creates trust and community, even with strangers. And it's changing the world in countless ways. ✳

Brave Action

Getting Good with Vulnerability

Start with yourself! This is harder than it sounds. We love to kid ourselves and pretend that everything is ok. That we're ok. Especially when we're not. It's time to be completely honest with yourself about what you want out of life. Why don't you already have it? How are your own actions preventing you from having what you want?

Then get vulnerable with a loved one. While I'm a big fan of getting out of your comfort zone, that's not the right place to start here. For this exercise I want you to find someone you are comfortable with and trust. Share one or more items from your personal list and ask them to share some of their own vulnerable experiences with you.

When you're standing in your vulnerable power, be sure to look people in the eye. Holding eye contact is one of the most physically awkward things ever and it's terribly hard to hide our vulnerability in those moments. Choosing to truly look at someone, to allow them to see your authentic, vulnerable self is one of the bravest things a person can do. It may feel extremely uncomfortable, perhaps even terrifying, but it can yield incredible results.

Expand and Empower

I'm quick to tell folks that there's no specific order to The BRAVE Method. You don't really have to follow it in the B-R-A-V-E order. Except for the last one. Expand and Empower. Because those aren't steps, they are the results of the first four letters.

If you do all of the previous steps, in any order you want, you will end up expanding and empowering yourself. It's just what happens. Because when we ask hard questions of ourselves and others, when we set boundaries, speak truths, get vulnerable, ask for help, and truly show up for ourselves we feel like complete badasses. We feel stronger, happier, more powerful. We even carry ourselves differently physically!

Think about it, when you do something you're proud of you stand taller, shoulders back, relaxed, smiling. There's an entire energy shift that happens in those moments and everyone in the room can feel it (yes, even if it's a virtual room).

When you're willing to create systems for regular reassessment of your goals, how you're spending your time and checking in with yourself on how you feel, day to day—you're truly growing. And you're growing in an intentional manner. You're in control. You have the power over your own life. You give yourself the gift of empowerment.

Empowerment. That's such a buzz word, isn't it!?

A lot of people talk about empowerment. In the entrepreneurial world I hear others say they "empower" audiences or clients all of the time and I'm here to tell you that's a total lie. No one can empower you. They can teach, guide, mentor, and inspire but the actions of empowerment…that's a gift only you can give yourself.

When you follow The BRAVE Method, you empower yourself.

When you show up for yourself and others, you empower yourself.

When you shut down your limiting voices and embrace the fears that tell you not to try, you empower yourself.

When you set boundaries, communicate them and stick to them, you empower yourself.

When you ask for help you empower yourself.

And all of this empowerment is what helps us expand into the person we want to be, into the business we want to run. Into the life we want to lead.

It's time to own your empowerment.

ALEXIA

Brave Spotlight

✳ Shedding Your "Perfect" Self

Perfectionism is often the antagonist in our life stories. It seeps into our core and rots us from the inside out. Perfectionism often halts our expansion and growth. It keeps us stuck, living small and afraid of taking risks.

As a child, Alexia Vernon loved to succeed—as long as the focus was on her accomplishments and not actually on her. It was important for Alexia to appear perfect. And that perfection was a well built wall that offered much desired protection.

Unfortunately, this mental dialogue and deep desire to "appear perfect" continued throughout most of her childhood. She loved to succeed but never wanted to be the center of attention or place herself in the spotlight. There was too much risk involved in that. Too many opportunities for others to see that she was not, in fact, perfect. Eventually however, and somewhat ironically, she found herself in the speaking circuit as a young adult. But even then, she viewed her speeches simply as good performances and continued to discredit her personal worth.

Over time, Alexia learned to surrender into her most authentic self. She began shedding the idea of "performing at her best" and embraced herself as she was. This didn't come without its challenges, of course. Alexia constantly battled between who she thought she was supposed to be and who she knew she was deep inside. And showing the parts that were deep inside was still a little too risky.

Many of us have faced a battle like this. It's easy to let society dictate our path. Allowing someone else to write your story takes a lot of pressure off. It's the easy way through life. But it's also the least effective and, by far, the least fun.

When I interviewed Alexia for *The Brave Files* podcast, she shared that after years of what she describes as "circling around the perimeter of her purpose" she decided to build the business she truly desired. It was time to trust herself and expand into the person she'd always been, the woman hiding underneath the surface of perfection. She and her husband began fully integrating their business and family life. They held strong to their core values, shifted their mindset, and stepped bravely down their new path.

Once Alexia cultivated the mindset and developed the habits to be able to work for herself, she became super passionate about showing up for others. Subsequently and unsurprisingly, her business blossomed! She now uses her own power to lead the way for other women, helping them to unapologetically use their own voices and find empowerment within. ✳

Brave Action

Empowerment

List out all the ways you've shown up for yourself in the last month. These can be anything from reading this book, eating healthy, allowing yourself to rest, taking a walk or a bubble bath, working out, making a sales call, writing, journaling, hiring a new team member or, even, firing a team member. Really think about *all* the ways you have been good to yourself. This list is proof that you're empowering yourself!

Now how about a little celebratory dance for your efforts and hard work?

PART TWO

Making It Happen

Understanding Your Habits

Be Radical

Now that I've walked you through The BRAVE Method, and given you actionable ways to begin implementing it in your life, I want to prepare you for a few things that might work against you as you dive, head first, into building the life of your dreams.

We are human, after all. That means we won't get it right every time and there's always going to be something that's extra hard or standing in your way. Being prepared for these eventualities is half the battle. You can fall off the wagon and get back on any time you wish. This isn't all or nothing. It's a repeated pattern of try something, fuck it up, try again, fuck up again, and keep going. The goal is, of course, to learn from each failure or mistake and continue to fail forward each time.

Let's explore some ways that life might throw you a curveball and how to best navigate them.

Understanding Your Habits

"Healthy habits are learned the same way as unhealthy ones—through practice."

- Wayne Dyer

How you spend your time matters.

You hear it all the time—"We all have the same number of hours in a day."

While this is totally true, we definitely do not all use those hours in the same way. Honestly, the way in which hours are spent is the main difference between those who live fulfilling lives and those who don't.

My mentor used to say to me, "How you do anything is how you do everything." While you may feel like you can squeeze in a Netflix binge, hours of social media scrolling, your overflow of work, and some quality time with the kids—you can't.

Some of you will believe that the more you can get done in a day the better. I'd venture to say many of you feel that way. But I ask you to consider this, if you're rushing to get "so much done" how many of those things are done well or accurately? You're most likely making mistakes because you're rushing, half-assing, or simply not paying enough attention to all that you're doing.

What if I told you that there was a way to get more time in your day? That there truly is an option to get lots of stuff done in one day, without multitasking? Guess what, you can. This is not a pipe dream! It just takes the right habits, commitments, and dedication to unlock this sought after level.

Want to know something interesting? Most of the time, you only feel zapped and stretched because you aren't managing your time effectively. You can actually fit way more into your day than it seems; you just aren't utilizing your time in a way that allows it.

I'm not terribly proud of the story I'm about to share but I am here to be completely honest with you, so, in the name of vulnerability let me go all in. A few weeks ago, I caught myself underprepared and stressed because there is no freaking way I was going to get "it all" done in time! The week was jam packed with product launches, book writing, school projects, podcasting, supporting my clients and, of course, raising four little girls (and the list goes on!) Now, I'm not trying to fool anyone. This is what most of my weeks look like. I am, after all, an entrepreneur, author, podcaster, partner, and a mother. There's always plenty of moving parts. But a few weeks ago I just let it all spiral out of control.

If you are anything like me, you want to do a good job with everything you do, but with your plate overflowing that seems nearly impossible. When things get this crazy it's easy to let overwhelm take over and just shut down. And you know what? Sometimes I do shut down. Not for long and not for good, but sometimes I have to step away from it all to regroup.

I'm betting that you, like me, have moments of feeling overwhelmed and underproductive. Days where it all catches up to you and you just feel low, low, low.

How many times have you found yourself so overwhelmed by your to-do list that, rather than being productive, you stare blankly at your social media feed? Or maybe your drug of choice is a Netflix binge. Personally, I say screw it and go for a pedicure—in fact, I did that yesterday. Whatever it is, clearly you are using your time in a way that doesn't align with your priorities. And a nasty side effect of misusing your time is knowing it and then there is that nasty feeling of shame that washes over you. *Ew.*

Do you feel like you're continuously running behind? Like you're playing a perpetual game of catch up? Do you see others that look like they have all of the time in the world and are still productive? Wondering why this can't be you?

It's time for some good news. This can, in fact, be you. By trying a few new things, creating some new habits, getting rid of some harmful habits, and being really honest with yourself, you can get out of this head game with yourself and really do some extraordinary things.

Right now I want you to sit and really think about your habits. What habits do you have that hinder you and which ones help you cross the finish line for each day successfully?

Creating Intentional Habits

When it comes to intentional habits, the most important thing to remember is this, keep your systems tight.

I've discovered that there are plenty of times in our lives where we feel compelled to throw all our systems out the window. Consider, for example, summer break for the work-at-home, entrepreneur, primary care providing parent like me. The struggle is *real* and there's a lot to manage to make it all work.

Typically, when we think of summer we picture idyllic, warm, sunny days playing and resting. That sounds lovely. But if you're an entrepreneur or industry leader, that might not be your reality.

Summer break is a much sought after time of connection and playfulness for kids and adults alike—or at least it's supposed to be. But it doesn't always feel that way to me. I am, after all, a single mother who owns three businesses and if I don't work, the bills don't get paid. There's nothing relaxing about that! But is there a middle ground? Can you carve out time to play and be in the moment with your family and still stay on top of things work wise? I say yes! The trick is to build and create intentional habits that are sustainable but also flexible.

Let's go on a little journey for a moment. Picture this: you're still your high achieving self with a roster full of clients. You're serving your people with power and passion, and you are allowing yourself time to relax and be in the peaceful space of fun and enjoyment for, at least part of, the summer. Sounds lovely, right? Well, it *is* lovely! And with a little forethought, preparation, and intentional planning, you can make it happen.

In our overworked society it takes a lot of intention to schedule time to relax. But if you don't prioritize and put intention around relaxation, connection, and self-care, the burnout will be real and fierce.

I've already shared that I work best at the last minute. I used to beat myself up, call myself a lazy procrastinator but the fact is I show up strongest when faced with a deadline. That doesn't mean, however, that I should completely sacrifice myself in these moments. By having strong boundaries, looking closely at my schedule, commitments, and deadlines I have a much higher success rate of accomplishing all that needs to be done while feeling a sense of harmony and balance at the same time. Does that mean it's never really stressful or challenging? Hell no! I still have those moments. But I also know exactly what I can do to prevent a total crash and burn.

I've been in that place where I pushed and crammed to meet a deadline. I was so committed and dedicated to a project that I was willing to sacrifice everything else around me. Once you start going down this rabbit hole, it's hard to see daylight! If you're anything like me, you begin to feel overwhelmed, underqualified, and like you're letting everyone, including yourself, down. When you get to that point nothing else matters. You may even feel like throwing in the towel completely. I wish I could help everyone prevent getting to this point of exhaustion because it really, truly does not have to be like this.

Creating habits that *honor you* in a 360 manner is key here! There are several, simple habits you can implement to help you define the boundaries between work and life. Many of these habits not only improve your work-life balance, but will also allow for additional growth within your work and life individually.

Get scheduled!

Work with a clear and intentional schedule rather than a vague to-do list. It doesn't matter if your summer hours are different from the rest of the year; identify them and build your life around them.

Get clear on your boundaries!

Intentionally focusing your time is great, but it's not possible without setting new boundaries. Identifying what boundaries are lacking in your life is the first step. If you attempt to set boundaries without spending quality, intentional time on them, you're likely to miss something, or more importantly you'll end up setting the wrong boundaries and this will move you further away from your goals rather than closer. We don't want that!

Identify when and if your boundaries might need to shift throughout the year.

Will you have special "summer boundaries?" How about during the holidays? Or when the kids go back to school? Building boundaries are habits that constantly need refining. Remember, once identified you have to follow through and clearly communicate them to others!

Be clear about your main professional priorities.

Do these priorities change throughout the year? What can you put in place, in advance, to allow for flexibility and movement in your business? Create a clear vision to action project list for achieving this.

Don't forget to make fun a habit!

Not prioritizing personal endeavors, fun, and family time is a dangerous habit to get into. Be sure to build these things in from the beginning because it's much easier than adding them in after the bottom falls out (but it's not impossible, more on that later).

Prioritize everything.

Once you identify your priorities, write them all out. Make a big long, healthy, old fashion list and then put a little spin on it! Lay everything on the table and start prioritizing tasks and events. I suggest organizing your list in one of two ways, but you can also experiment and find a system that works best for you.

1. Organize by importance
2. Organize by ease

Personally, I use both systems! I start by prioritizing importance and then I break that down even further and organize the low hanging fruit in each sub category. What's most important is not losing sight of my intention! When you always understand why you're doing something and what result you want from it you'll feel more confident and in control. This will trickle down into every other element of your life in a magical way.

Intentional self-care.

Look friends—this is a marathon not a sprint. We have to train in slow, intentional, actionable steps to complete the race and taking a break is not time wasted. In fact, it's required to take planned, intentional breaks. Without them you will crash and burn in every way possible. Without intentional time for yourself, you become fatigued, exhausted, and you begin to experience tunnel vision. Taking a step back gives you a good reset and a fresh perspective.

So often this is a space we find ourselves being reactionary. If this is your approach you're probably stressed out, overworked, under cared for, and ready to just throw in the towel. Instead of treating self-care as reactionary, I'm suggesting you be proactive about it. That means taking small, intentional steps to prioritize caring for yourself every single day.

Build free time into your schedule.

By scheduling this free time into your calendar, you're giving yourself permission to step away and honor your personal needs. Trust me; I've been there too. Without a designated time scheduled for unplugging and relaxing, you'll easily lose focus and end up facing some serious burnout.

This free time may look different for many of you. It could be just setting aside a few minutes to mediate or sit in silence. Perhaps it's a walk around the block, practicing a mantra, writing out gratitude, journaling, throwing a load of laundry in or a quick check on Twitter (my personal favorite). *The one thing it is, for sure, is your time to do as you please.*

And yes, I'm suggesting this free time be scheduled into your normal work day. I also suggest you allow this to be a creative action when you're feeling too much pressure or stuck on something. A change of scenery and pace has the ability to unleash some powerful new ideas.

If you apply all of these ideas and implement them into your daily or weekly schedule, you'll find that sense of balance and harmony are indeed possible. With the right self-care habits in place, your stress and anxiety will decrease—it's just science!

I completely recognize this is hard to do! When I was pushing and cramming for deadlines, I experienced such a total state of burnout that I could hardly hold a conversation with anyone in my personal life without wanting to cry or shout. I thought I managed my workload fairly well (although clearly something wasn't up to par there either because when we're totally broken it appears in every part of our life) but there was, literally, nothing left of me outside of work. I needed some serious sacred rest (as referenced in the radical self-care section of the book). I had to slow myself down and take a look at how I was moving through my days and weeks. How was I spending my time and what needed to change. It was space for myself that was missing. Without a designated time scheduled for unplugging and relaxing, you'll easily lose focus and end up facing some serious burnout. This recognition is what, eventually, led to my now treasured solo-retreats.

These intentional habits apply to your home life as well. Be dedicated to the life around you and not distracted by work. Work has its time, but your wellbeing, your family, and your friends deserve their time too. Sometimes rest is the bravest action you can take.

While all of this may sound simple, let me assure it's not. Don't make the mistake of assuming this is "easy" or not a big deal. It's a big fucking deal. Being intentional with your time can literally change your life. True intention is formed through creating habits, dedicating yourself to the goal (personal or professional), and learning to set firm boundaries. And they are absolutely fucking worth it.

Don't Sell Yourself Short

I love to read. Books are sacred in my house and they're piled on top of multiple bookshelves, surfaces, and even the floor. When I was pregnant with my oldest daughter I began a book collection for her that was over 100 books deep before she was even born. Each night, I read to her, still inside my belly, the same two or three books so she would recognize the cadence of my voice and the rhythm of the words. I even recited the words from *Goodnight Moon* the first time I held her in my arms. I'm still convinced she knew exactly who I was and what I was saying as she stared into my eyes that very first time. And I can recite the book even now.

We even have the most magical little free library in our front yard. Lovingly hand painted by the kids, welcoming anyone and everyone to take a book or leave a book. Watching families walk by and dig through for a little treasure is such a joy. Seeing folks from all walks of life look for a book, or go out of their way to fill up the library with books they are no longer reading creates for unexpected and beautiful conversations. It builds community in a way that little else can, in my opinion.

But I didn't always love to read. I didn't even pick up a book, for pleasure, until I was in middle school and my aunt introduced me to romance novels. You read that right, at the wise old age of twelve I cut my reading teeth on heteronormative historical romance novels with half naked people on the cover and bosoms spilling over corsets. But hey, that was also the beginning of my love affair with history so that has to count for something, right?! But it wasn't until my High School English tutor, Laura, gave me a copy of Betty Smith's *A Tree Grows in Brooklyn* that I fell in love with reading. I'm not exactly sure what it was about the beloved American classic about a young girl's coming-of-age at the turn of the century, that so spoke to the very core of me, but it did.

The gloves were off after that. I was obsessed with literature and writing. I was so into it that I took five elective English classes my senior year in High School. I still, on occasion, share my favorite book reads with my High School English teacher, Joan, which is something that brings me immense joy. I then went on to get an English degree in college. And as a young college grad, I spent a great deal of my free time reading.

And then life took over. I started a business, got married, and became a mother. I quickly fell into the trap that so many parents find themselves in. I loved the idea of reading but there simply wasn't any time. Even if there was time I was too damn tired to use it for reading.

I also had this tired old story that I simply couldn't read unless I had hours at a time to dedicate to the book. I let this bullshit story mess with my head for a very long time.

I was in this way too busy, non-reading phase for over twelve years. The idea of ever being able to pick up a book again seemed nearly impossible. And then in early January 2019 Casee Marie, a woman I had interviewed for the *The Brave Files* podcast and had become friends with, nominated me to participate in the twelve books in twelve months challenge.

The challenge was to select twelve books that have been sitting on your shelves, collecting dust, and commit to reading one a month. In theory, that should be simple enough. But come on! I hadn't read twelve pages in the previous year. How in the world was I supposed to read twelve books? So I said no. Boundaries, right!? We don't have to say yes to everything!

But this reading challenge stayed on my mind. I missed reading. I felt like something was missing in my life without reading on a regular basis. I started to wonder "was I really too busy?' I felt like this would be an almost impossible commitment to keep, and yet I was called to it. It was as if my soul knew I needed this.

I also knew that nearly every successful person I know is an avid reader. And then I read an article where President Barack Obama shared his favorite fifty books from the previous year.

Come on Heather, I thought to myself. If President Obama can read 50–100 books a year, surely you can read twelve!

I believe that learning is powerful, and reading is learning. I wanted to do this. I started to believe that I could do it. So I sat in front of my book shelves. They were covered in books that I'd been interested in but never given myself permission to read. I lovingly and thoughtfully selected twelve books that had been growing dust on my shelf and committed to reading one book each month.

But there was a catch. I knew this wouldn't be possible without some new habits and a lot of intention. So I set to work identifying what habits I wanted to change to make way for the new ones.

First, I decided to keep a book on hand and whenever I had a few minutes to kill I would read rather than scroll through social media. This has worked shockingly well. Second, I committed to reading, at least a little bit, every single day and even scheduled fifteen minutes of reading time in my work day. This gave me permission to read and not feel like I was slacking off.

In the last few days of 2019, the year I accepted the twelve books in twelve months challenge, I finished reading my thirty-fourth book for the year. That was nearly three times the goal I'd set for myself and it felt incredible. In 2020 I read fifty-four books! That's four and a half books a month and it had all seemed so impossible when I started. As of the publication of this book I have read over 80 books and counting!

When I first accepted the reading challenge, I tried to be specific and intentional about which books I read and in what order.

That proved to be a little difficult because my moods and interests would vary. I felt a little constricted by this self-imposed boundary. So in 2020 I chose to read whatever I wanted and just flow with it. For 2021 I've changed it up again and I suspect this is the system that will stick.

These days I have three books going at once. The old me, the one that believed she had to have hours and hours of free time to read, wouldn't even know what to do with herself! She was convinced she could only read one book at a time. Ha! I'm sticking my tongue out at my past, self-constrained, self and reminding her that there are lots of ways she can grow.

Here's how I've successfully broken down my reading. I always have three books going at once:

- Personal or professional development book that I read in the mornings on weekdays or when I have a few free minutes during the work day (rather than scrolling through social media).

- Audio book that I listen to in the car, in the shower, while doing chores, or when out walking alone. These are typically memoirs because I really enjoy listening to people tell their stories.

- Fiction book that brings me pleasure to read in the evenings and on the weekends.

Creating or changing a few small habits can make an incredible difference. And I am giddy with joy at all of the learning and reading pleasure I've allowed back into my life.

CARLA

Brave Spotlight

✳ Avoiding the Crash

We never know what the Universe holds for us, but one thing is for sure: If we're not careful, our lives can be on a collision course towards disaster. Take Carla Moore for example. Carla was a powerhouse executive whose life nearly ended during a tragic car accident. Surviving a nearly unsurvivable crash not only gave Carla a second chance at life but also paved a new way for clarity and awareness.

Prior to the crash, Carla was uncomfortable with her weight of 350 pounds, had no real sense of purpose, and she was confused. She'd followed the path that was set up for her. Gone to college and received her MBA, moved away from home, gotten a good job with HBO—and here she was at 40-years-old, unhealthy and with no inward goals.

When she awoke at the hospital, after her accident, and realized she wanted a higher purpose for herself and her life, Carla made herself four promises. She was determined to lose a hundred pounds, run a 5K, renew her involvement in community service and outreach, and visit Rome! Once she made these declarations, she began to develop a plan to check each item off the list, one by one. With deep thoughtfulness and intention, Carla set upon her new path.

Many of us struggle with achieving goals and that's why Carla created a goal implementation plan that would be easy to follow and, as she would soon discover, actually works. How do we reach our own lofty goals without giving up? Carla says you have to be ready to "accept no other alternative" and stick to a daily routine. She had to alter old habits and create new ones in order to live the new life she dreamed of!

"You start by visualizing your goal and actually seeing the outcome," Carla says, "then you educate yourself, and finally, *you* do the work!" It sounds easy...but we all know it isn't. Carla reminds us that "transformation is not for the weak." But it's totally achievable! She starts each day with gratitude and personal mantras. Then, throughout the day she visualizes and pictures the outcome of her goals. At the beginning of her transformation, she bought a treadmill and started tracking her diet.

Amazingly, but not surprisingly, within a year Carla reached her weight loss goal, ran a 5k, and took a trip to Rome. She also became more involved with her sorority outreach and set up regular donations to the Red Cross.

To Carla's surprise, there were some wonderful and unexpected results of her personal transformation. She started to notice how things began to flow into other parts of her life. Suddenly, the journey for personal clarity became contagious and her newfound confidence propelled her professional career. Eventually, she began speaking at conferences and leadership seminars then, one day something magical happened—Carla was approached with a book deal.

Her clever and effective book *Crash: Leading Through The Wreckage, Using Personal Transformation to Transform Your Leadership* was born.

During her engaging interview on *The Brave Files* podcast, Carla and I discuss a truly powerful question: As you begin to reach your goals, how do you stay the course? As Carla says before the crash she was "looking straight ahead and not seeing anything." We must choose to be present and grounded, stand in gratitude, and celebrate our successes. But, "be enlightened enough to know when you are off track." You have to learn to remove yourself from temptations and lean on family and friends. "When you get a sense of who you are, and what you're here to do, you move with that force and that power to help create the life that you've imagined." ✳

You Have to Do the Work!

I want to make something very, very clear. None of this is magic. It doesn't happen by accident or because you simply will it into being. It takes work. Hard, intentional work.

Interestingly enough, one of the first books in the twelve months reading challenge was *The Power of Habit* by Charles Duhigg. Through an easy to understand formula, and a lot of really fantastic case studies, Duhigg shows us exactly how to identify unhealthy habits and change them.

Here is Duhigg's habit pattern:

Cue → Routine → Reward[1]

If you change any of these three elements, you can alter or create a new habit.

Once habits are formed, they are often difficult to change. But not at all impossible to change! Some become so routine that we don't even realize we're doing them, like brushing our teeth or driving to the office.

Other (new) habits are easily formed. Take remembering to water your houseplants, for example. You may not think about it the moment you get home, but you leave the watering can next to the kitchen sink. When you see it there, you remember, "Oh! I have to water the plants!" Use that same example to think through your day. How many easy solutions are there to creating habits like this one?

The same tactic worked for me with reading. Anytime I had a few minutes free and the urge to pick up my phone and scroll through social media popped up, I would pick up my book. I changed one of the three elements Duhigg teaches (what action I took when I had the urge to scroll through social media) and that helped me create a new, sustainable habit.

Let's imagine you want to start taking a healthy snack to the office, so you prep it the night before and leave a note on your bag for the next morning. Want to start turning off your electronics an hour before you head to bed? Set an alarm on your phone as a reminder. These are simple habits. They may not come naturally at first, but they have easy solutions you can implement immediately.

Other habits take more work. These would be things like time blocking your days to produce content more effectively, quitting the constant email checking that's keeping you on the hamster wheel all day long, creating boundaries for your own sanity, or ditching the distractions of social media. Changing your habits in these areas is going to require a more dedicated approach.

One way I've discovered to make a habit truly stick is to dive deep when planning it out. Instead of just deciding which habit you'll work on, you will decide when, how, and where you'll do it. I've found it's better to complete the activity at the same time and in the same place every time. It's kind of like brushing your teeth every morning. You wouldn't leave your toothbrush in the living room, would you? You keep it near the sink where you brush your teeth. The same thing goes for every other habit you form. Decide where it makes most sense, and commit to repeating the action for as long as it continues to move you closer to your goals.

Reward Yourself

Just like our routines and boundaries, if we're not careful, our habits can get out of control fast. If we're not intentional and thoughtful, we develop habits we don't want and that don't serve our greater visions. I suggest checking in with your habits as often as you check in with your commitments. Are your habits moving you closer to your goals? Are they serving you? Do they feel good?

I have a client who struggles to drink enough water throughout the day. She knows skipping water makes her sluggish and feel bad but she simply cannot seem to drink enough water. I also know she loves a good reward, even something as small as a sticker! So we created little stickers for her to put up for each cup of water she drinks. Seeing those stickers makes her excited and proud and it motivates her to drink more water. These tricks don't have to be complicated. Keep trying new approaches until you find something that works for you. Check in on those habits and build in a rewards system to go along with it!

Brave Action

Remember Creating Habits Takes Time

As nice as it would be—new, healthier habits are not born overnight.

Tracking your habits (especially the ones you don't want to keep) is the best place to start. Remember, once we're aware of our behavior things start to shift quickly. It's exciting and powerful to track your progress. This works with goals and habits!

Pick one habit, one thing that you know will move you further down the path toward your goals? Decide which of Duhigg's elements you want to shift (cue, routine, reward) and then give it a try. Whatever the habit may be, track it for a week or two and see what happens! Believe me, you *will* see a payoff. Before you know it, this action will be second nature.

When tracking habits, take note of the following:

- What is your intention?
- Where and when will you complete the habit?
- Have you done as you intended daily?
- Are you getting the desired result?

In fact, I have a tracking sheet template to share with you. The link is in the reference guide at the back of the book. This is a great tool that helps you, literally, check your habits off as you complete them. It's a daily assessment, and it's one that makes all the difference in terms of real growth. Even after years of completing this exercise, it feels rewarding to see those check marks build up. I'll tell you, knowing you're on the track to living life the way you want is a powerful feeling. It truly can change your entire perspective!

And don't forget to plan out a reward for keeping up with this new habit for a month. Rewards are serious motivation. I promise you, hard work does pay off!

Be Radical

Radical Self-compassion

I was first introduced to Dr. Kristin Neff's work on self-compassion in a podcast interview. I didn't really pay attention to the work at the time because I felt like I had a good handle on self-compassion. I took breaks when I needed them, shut down my limiting voices (most of the time) and took "good care" of myself.

When I finally started to dig deeper into what it meant to really be self-compassionate, I was surprised to find there was much in there for me to learn. I'd been confusing self-esteem and self-care with self-compassion. And, as I'd eventually come to know, they are really quite different.

Much like my research in gratitude, the concept of self-compassion felt intangible and "woo woo" but it turns out it's science, plain and simple. Who would have thought that leading a more self-compassionate life would lead to a healthier and more productive life? That it would enable me to be more resilient and to give more to others, in the long run? That by showing myself compassion I'd become more stable, less scattered and less stressed?

But that's what I learned to do once I began exploring self-compassion. Discovering that I could comfort myself, validate myself and "hold" myself in tenderness and grace has been life changing. It allows me to catch myself right at my breaking point, pause, reflect and then get up and try again.

What Dr. Neff's research has proven is that our minds cannot tell the difference between kind words and support from an outside source vs ourselves. Our parasympathetic nervous system doesn't know if someone else is gently rubbing our arms in comfort or if we're doing it ourselves.

I'll admit, I thought it all sounded ridiculous at first but speaking to myself in kind, compassionate ways, and giving myself physical comfort, has truly changed the way I move through my life.

Just the other day I was in the car with my teenage daughter and a car nearly hit us. I was so upset and frightened that I was on the verge of road rage. Because of my self-compassion training, I instantly went into self-compassion mode and started talking softly and gently to myself saying, "It's ok, Heather. It's totally normal to be scared and angry when someone puts you and your child's life at risk. Your reaction is human." From there I quickly started to calm down. I could, literally, feel my blood pressure lower and my breathing go back to normal.

Now, don't get me wrong, my daughter looked at me like I was nuts. But I casually said, "I'm showing myself some self-compassion," and went on driving. I wonder what type of long term, positive effects, seeing me treat myself compassionately will have on my girls. Energy is, after all, contagious.

While there are several exercises you can do to teach yourself how to tap into self-compassion (and I highly recommend you read

Kristin's book!), here are a few that will begin to open up the study to you. They are easy to do and will have a tremendous impact.

- Ask yourself "would I treat a friend this way?" If the answer is no, then don't treat yourself that way.

- Give yourself a supportive touch by rubbing your own arms or neck. Gently hold your abdomen or place your hand over your heart while you breathe deeply.

- Reframe your inner dialogue to be one of kindness and compassion. Love is a far better motivator than fear.

Remember that self-compassion is about allowing ourselves to feel whatever we're experiencing *without casting judgement.* It's not about pretending we're not in pain or experiencing anger. It's about letting it in, because it's a natural human emotion (just like fear!), and then deciding what we want to do about it.

Radical Self-trust

Learning to trust yourself is like having a magic wand. But it's not easy and takes a lot of work! We all go through periods of significant shifts in our lives. Times where everything seems to get out of place and then back into a new "normal" position. To put it simply, these times are a period of true awakening. It can feel disconcerting and outrageously uncomfortable, perhaps even painful. Especially if we're resisting the changes that we have little control over. These changes, or growth opportunities depending on your perspective, appear in many ways from how you conduct yourself professionally to the ways in which you move through your personal life. During the pandemic and this time of significant uncertainty, stress, and forced stillness, we had the opportunity to learn something new. For many, it's been an eye-opening experience, and I am no exception. If you're really paying attention to what's happening in and around you, being honest, utilizing The BRAVE Method, and reflecting, you'll likely discover that after a forced change, such as we all experienced during the pandemic, there is much we lost that we don't want back. Yes, there is a lot to miss but as I've watched my clients and loved ones restructure their lives and businesses, I've noticed that we've all become far more creative in how we problem solve. While everyone could have just shut down and given up, that's not what happened. We have the ability to build a new future for ourselves that leaves behind the things we discovered are not serving us.

In the beginning of lockdown I hit the pause button for about six weeks. I was overwhelmed and burnt out. Life was moving both at warp speed and at a snail's pace. I truly couldn't find my stride. I was at a loss. I'm the one who's supposed to coach, encourage, and motivate, right?! Yes, but I'm still human, and it all felt like too much.

But once I gave myself permission to slow down, everything changed.

"Once I gave myself permission to slow down, everything changed."

I didn't feel guilty, and I was finally able to get back on track with what mattered the most to me. Alignment happened when I told myself it was okay to pause. Once I embraced it all—the challenges, the emotions, the adjustments, and the learning curve—I was able to find my groove again. I recharged, and then I took action. *But here's a little secret, sometimes I need to go back to pause—and I have learned to let that be ok!*

And you know what? It was exactly what I needed. Now I'm able to step up and discover new ways to support those around me. I'm working with clients as they make significant changes to their businesses. It's been intense, but it's been worth it.

As I continue to connect to gratitude and intertwine myself even more deeply with my community, I'm reflecting on what this season of life is teaching me. Sometimes it's hard to focus on the lessons amidst the struggle, but I know it's important.

So here we are. Strong, committed, diving in, even without a clear destination in mind, and moving forward. There are a few things I've learned to fall back on with certainty.

There's value in learning to trust yourself.

Trust is a heavy word, but it's vital when focusing on living with intention. How can you move forward in a way that brings you peace when you don't fully trust you're heading in the right direction? That's a loaded question, for sure, but it brings something super important to the forefront. *You have to learn to trust yourself.*

When life feels uncertain or things feel especially challenging, you can't always trust what's happening around you. This is where trusting in your *own* abilities and intuition comes into play. When it comes to your life, *you* are the constant. Working to grow that trust in yourself—above all else—is the way to go. If you ask me, it's the ultimate form of bravery because many of us are told, from the time we're small, that we lack the ability to trust ourselves or make good decisions for ourselves.

I was raised with a helicopter mom. She paid extremely close attention to what I was doing and was invested in my success being what she felt was the "right kind" of success. That's the reason

I joined a sorority in college—because my mom wanted me to. It's why I didn't drive on the freeway as a teenager—my mom didn't think it was safe. It wasn't until I was 38 and came out that I stopped allowing my mother to dictate what was deemed successful. Don't get me wrong, I'm not blaming my mom. She loved me and was doing what she thought was best but having someone you respect and admire in your life dictate your actions doesn't breed a strong foundation for self-trust. This is a fact I have to constantly remind myself of when it comes to my own children. If I guide all of their decisions they won't ever believe they have what it takes to trust themselves. The same goes for my clients. My job isn't to give them the answers, it's to help them realize they have all the answers they need within. It's my job to help them learn to listen to and trust themselves.

Since making the brave decision to live my own, authentic life I've gained so much more respect from my mom. It seems that all I needed to do to get her to trust me was to advocate for myself. Why do we do that? Why do we allow others to run the show, even when we know they aren't making the decisions that are right for us?

I know that my mom's intentions were always good. She was doing the best she could. There's no parenting guidebook. But putting yourself in charge of everyone's choices is not a healthy way to raise a human.

And now parents have moved from being helicopter parents to lawn mower parents. They just mow down anything in the way of their child's success. This is such a dangerous situation to be in because kids never, ever, learn to work hard for something. They don't learn that they can't have everything they want and sometimes we lose and they sure as hell don't learn to trust themselves!

As a parent I know how hard it is to watch my kids fail or not get something they really want but I also know that, in the long run, it's the best option for them. I'm still a momma bear and will take you out if you harm one of my children. But I let them make their own decisions as much as possible so that they can then reap the rewards, or consequences.

I'm doing everything in my power to raise four young women who trust themselves. Society makes this a difficult endeavor but I started by not getting involved in their clothing choices once they were old enough to have an opinion. Same with hair, music, books. I let them have control over their decision about almost anything as long as they're not in harm's way. I challenged myself, early on in my parenting journey, to say "yes" whenever possible. If I didn't have a really good reason to say no, it was a yes. And sometimes that's hard. Having a house full of decisive, strong willed girls is the ultimate challenge. But if we want our children to trust themselves, we must trust them first!

If you're a business owner with employees, this same concept rings true. If you want dedicated, passionate, hardworking team members, you have to trust them to do the job you hired them to do! If they make a mistake then deal with it case by case. But people who are enabled, empowered and trusted make braver and more audacious choices that will, almost always, pay off for your company. Nothing risked, nothing gained! There may be some failing now and again but if you're never failing, you're never trying.

It's time to trust yourself in a really radical way. Stop asking for approval or justification from others. You know what's right for you, your family, and your business, so trust that you will pull through.

Allow yourself space for rest, quiet, and reflection.

This is a big one. Space is a necessary component of finding balance. It's nearly impossible to maintain a positive and determined mindset in life when you don't allow yourself time to simply be present. It's certainly easy to get caught up in growth or fighting for an important cause, but every human needs rest—I've learned this the hard way. It's hard to power through when you feel like you have nothing left in the tank.

And finally, give yourself grace.

It's okay to do nothing sometimes, and you don't need to feel guilty about it! You're human, and you're doing the best you can. If you stumble, take a moment to look around. Think about where you are and where you've been. Then use that to make a plan for where you'll go.

It's worth noting that just this past summer I had the privilege of being in the *exact same position as my own mother* when my oldest daughter got her driver's license. I was so proud of her. She's a great driver and takes that responsibility very seriously. However, she's a bit timid and merging off and on the expressway is particularly challenging for her. Once she was a legal driver, I told her she couldn't drive on the expressway because she wasn't confident enough in herself and I was afraid there would be an accident. She agreed and understood. And then about a week later I realized I was making the same mistake my mom had made. So we revised the rule, she would do the expressway driving with me for a few more weeks to get comfortable with merging and then I would trust her to do it on her own. And by giving my trust, she would learn to, hopefully, trust herself. The surrender is sometimes as hard as the trust. But it's worth it. No one's journey is perfect, and that's okay. It's important to be gentle with yourself. Grace is for everyone.

Voices in Your Head

In order to lean into radical self-trust you have to face off with your limiting voices. Those little assholes are keeping you from the next big thing.

Do you know what your limiting voices are? Some of you can, likely, call out those pain in the ass voices right away. But many of you will need to do some work in order to identify them and decide if you want to give them residence in your head and life!

How many times a day do you hear a voice inside your head telling you some crazy story that slows you down? Those stories *feel* real. More often than not, we believe them. The truth is, though, that most of those stories are bullshit. Seriously, they are rooted in fear and not based on reality.

Our perception creates our reality. That means that the internal conversations we have with ourselves carry a lot of weight. They have the power to knock us down or lift us up. In most cases, the "limiting" voices give us reasons why something won't work, why we are not good enough, why no one will listen anyway. I am here to tell you these voices are lying and I can prove it!

I am willing to bet you have some of the same limiting voices I have and the same ones many of my clients have. Here are just a few that I see all the time.

"I don't have what it takes"

"No one wants to hear what I have to say"

"No one wants to buy what I have to sell"

"I have to work 24/7 to be successful"

"I don't know HOW to do it"

"I just can't do it"

"It's not the right time"

"I am too good for this"

"I am not good enough for this"

"I'm a fraud"

And my personal favorite is "I don't work hard enough." This is the one that I constantly hear in my head all the damn time. I *believe* in designing balance for my life. I've spent years building my life the way I want it and I am damn good at implementing the necessary boundaries and systems that make it work for me. But that doesn't stop that nasty little limiting voice from telling me "I don't work hard enough" when I don't work every second of the day, or sacrifice sleep and time for myself and my family. I mean, I'm an entrepreneur! Work is always sitting in front of my face. My brain says "you should be constantly working. Always. If you're not, then you're not working hard enough you asshole." These voices *suck*. They make us feel less than and they give us permission to not push through.

The question is what to do about them? How do you shut them up faster, if not permanently? You do the work to prove they are full of shit and you keep that evidence close by! When my inner voice says "I don't work hard enough" I like to reference a pretty kick ass list I keep called my "truth about me" list. It has my clients listed, the conferences and workshops I have been invited to speak at, positive feedback from my clients and anything that can disprove the voices and show me the truth! I *do* work hard enough and part of why I work so hard is to enjoy the personal side of the balance I've built. The "evidence" those voices are trying to use against me is exactly how I know my plan is working. So that inner voice can suck it!

To change your inner conversation and remove those dreaded limiting voices, you first have to identify them. Once you've identified them and you're aware of just how often they present themselves, you'll discover that changing the behavior happens much more quickly.

When you combine awareness with intention you're able to take brave action and create new habits. Remember when I told you about the twelve books in twelve months challenge? I told you I found the time for reading in the "cracks" of my life but what I didn't tell you was the limiting voice that always appeared when I thought about taking on a reading challenge like that. The voice said "You can't read that much, it's too hard and you're not disciplined enough. Besides, you don't have the time. If you read you won't be working and then you'll be letting everyone down!"

But I knew how to change a habit, thanks to Charles Duhigg's *The Power of Habit* and I'm now aware of how often this nagging voice presents itself. So I created a new dialogue around it. Each fifteen minute sprint was a win. Each book finished meant I did have time, I was disciplined enough and learning was an important part of doing my job well!

I've talked to some people who read over a hundred books a year and others have said they can't read twelve pages in an entire year! What I have accomplished feels extraordinary to me. I'm terribly proud and also a whole lot smarter because the more we learn the more we know and reading is an awesome way to learn.

KAREN

Brave Spotlight

✳ Flip Time on Its Head

Some of our most dangerous and powerful limiting voices are around how much time we have, or think we have. Author and creator of *Flip Time*, Karen Briscoe, told me when I interviewed her for *The Brave Files* podcast that we can change our lives if we reframe how we think about time. Instead of thinking about time in terms of minutes, Karen says, "It's more a matter of focus and energy. It's your energy, not your time, that's a fundamental currency of high performance." She cites Parkinson's Law, which states that limiting or restricting time can help you become more effective and efficient. Ultimately, Karen says, when we say we don't have enough time what we're saying is we don't want to. When we want to do it badly enough, we make time.

Karen helps people unpack their limiting beliefs about time because she knows that our perceptions of the world shape our realities in powerful ways. In college, she internalized the popular thought that women could only be either career women or housewives. Karen's someone who gets tremendous personal fulfillment from her career, but she also wanted a family. She felt trapped. She chose to work part-time so she could start a family. Like many of us, she began to measure her life in milestones: When [x] happens, then I can finally do [y]. "I feel like I was on the path I was supposed to be on, but I didn't pursue it wholeheartedly," Karen says. "I pursued it with a spirit of lack rather than abundance. Instead of seeing the good in what I was doing, I was always looking at what I wasn't doing because I was doing something else." Unlearning these beliefs was difficult work but she managed to flip the script. Now, she pursues her life—all facets of her life—with a spirit of abundance.

Karen says it's not enough to just "get through the day." The goal is to thrive rather than simply surviving. You deserve to be able to enjoy the life you're living while building the life of your dreams. ✳

Brave Action

Limiting Voices

Write down your limiting voices.

Spend some time for the next two to three days being really aware of them. What are the stories and when do they get in your way? Write them out!

After you create this list and start to notice just how often these little buggers creep into your mind, I want you to play a little game with them. I want you to "turn them around" by writing out the polar opposite of each limiting voice. Again, you don't have to believe the opposite is true, just play along and write it down.

Then, after you've written the turnarounds, look for evidence to disprove each of these limiting voices and create your own "truth about me" list. Utilize your truth about me list as often as possible. Read it in the morning, reflect on it at night, journal about it, share it with others and pull it out whenever you need a little emotional or motivational boost.

Here are some examples of ways to think through your limiting voices, create turnarounds and find evidence in your own life and business to prove the turnarounds right:

Limiting Voices	Turn-arounds	Sample Evidence
I don't have what it takes	I do have what it takes	I have clients who pay to hear what I have to say
No one wants to hear what I have to say	People do want to hear what I have to say	My schedule is booked with paying clients
No one wants to buy what I have to sell	People buy what I sell	I have created valuable products that make a difference in peoples lives
I have to work 24/7 to be successful	I can have boundaries around my work hours and be successful	When I create and communicate healthy boundaries others react positively and learn to do the same
I don't know HOW to do it	I have resources available to help me figure out anything I need to know	I've utilized resources, mentors, teachers, and guides to help me learn
I'm not ready yet	I am as ready as I'll ever be	If I always waited to be ready, I wouldn't have achieved anything in my life
I don't work hard enough	I work hard enough	I have paying clients. We have more than enough of all that we need

Radical Self-care

Self-care is a total buzz word these days. Many people I know have started to actually cringe when they see it. It's been commercialized and bastardized so much that we no longer really even understand what it means.

But self-care isn't a joke and it's not just for "other people." *Self-care must be for you.* I consider it the Oxygen Mask Effect! You know how, when you get on an airplane they tell you "in case of an emergency" you should put *your* mask on before helping others with theirs? That's what I'm talking about. We live in a world where we're constantly being told to put others' needs before our own. Even if those words aren't spoken, it's implied. This is especially true for women and mothers. And *working* mothers. Holy shit are they expected to be superhuman. But we're not superhuman. We're just as human as the next person and when we try to give and give and give without ever making time to grow ourselves, love ourselves, and care for ourselves—we eventually break.

As I mentioned before, one way I've started combating this deep level of exhaustion and burnout is by taking quarterly solo retreats. What started out as a thirty hour, unplugged, solo getaway has developed into a full blown personal retreat schedule. Sometimes these retreats are working but often they are just about reconnecting with myself, listening to myself, and decompressing.

I've learned over the years, and it was made even more abundantly clear during the pandemic when shelter in place started, that I require alone time to be healthy. I'm a single mom of four, a partner, a success coach, and a podcast producer and host. I give my time and energy all day long. Don't get me wrong, this is all by choice. I *love* my job, my clients, my kids and my partner, but I reach a point where I can no longer even be in the same energetic space as someone else because it sucks too much out of me. I feel like a deflated balloon who everyone wants to still be flying high and beautiful.

It took me a long time to realize that, as an empath, just being in the same building as other people zaps my energy. I am in the business of giving, and I love it. But in order to keep giving to my clients, my kids, my partner, and everyone else—I've learned to have regular scheduled maintenance for "giving" to myself. And I love these solo retreats. I often go four or five days without even speaking to another person. For someone who makes a living talking to people from stages, on podcasts and in coaching sessions, this forced quiet is lifesaving.

So, going to a hotel alone for a few days, even if it's to get some work done, is total self-care for me. When I'm not working I can do whatever I want and I don't have to share energy with others. I take these solo trips at least three or four times a year. Sometimes I just get a hotel or rent an airbnb nearby, sometimes I travel or add a few days to a trip I've taken for work. But it's become an important decompression ritual for me. More often than not, I use this time just to be with myself. To walk around, read a lot and sit in silence. Sometimes I work on specific projects, like this book. Typically I pick different locations within a couple hours of home, pack my car full of food for several days and a giant pile of books and tell my people I love them but don't call unless there's a serious emergency. I always stick to myself and enjoy my time alone.

I realize this is a privileged thing to be able to do. To afford the hotel and the time away is a gift. Mind you, it's a gift I work hard to afford and it's something I make a priority, but it's still a privilege. When I'm not able to get away I find time "in the cracks" to care for myself.

Here are some of my favorite, at home, self-care options.

- Lots of walks

- Deep breathing and stretching in the morning

- Morning affirmations and declarations

- A hot cup of tea or coffee

- Prioritizing a real, sit down launch for myself in the middle of a work day

- Taking a gratitude break

- Having a 10–15 minute power nap

- Reading for a few minutes

- Doing thirty jumping jacks

- The Wonder Woman Pose for two to three minutes

- Essential oils

- Finding the sun spot in my house and sitting in it for a few minutes

SAUNDRA

BravE Spotlight

✳ Change Your Life with Sacred Rest

A couple of years ago I was introduced to Dr. Saundra Dalton-Smith who I was lucky enough to interview for *The Brave Files* podcast. Dr. Dalton-Smith is a board-certified internal medicine physician. She actively sees and treats patients but her approach to medicine has completely shifted in the last few years after she experienced debilitating and terrifying personal burnout. Dr. Dalton-Smith knows first hand that self-care is vitally important to living a healthy life.

Once she knew that her physical ailments weren't due to any specific medical conditions she began to realize it was total and complete burn out. Being the practical thinker she is, Dr. Dalton-Smith knew her choices and actions had gotten her into this mess and that meant they could also get her out of it!

I learned from her that rest is about intention (see, I told you at the beginning of this book that intention was the core component required for making the brave leap!). Rest, Dr. Dalton-Smith says, is giving a truthful no instead of a reluctant yes. It's taking a break during your workday and enjoying the world around you. And, it's so much more than getting a good night's sleep. Dr. Dalton-Smith identified seven types of "sacred rest" required to live our heaviest lives.

Physical

Mental

Spiritual

Emotional

Social

Sensory

Creative

I've personally learned when my body and soul is craving sacred rest. It's not just being tired, it's more like feeling broken and hopeless even though things are, technically, going well. By combining scientific research with personal stories, spiritual insight, and practical next steps, sacred rest gives the weary permission to embrace rest, set boundaries, and seek sanctuary without any guilt, shame, or fear.

I hope you'll decide to implement The BRAVE Method in every possible area of your life, including knowing yourself well enough to seek the rest you need. *

Radical Authenticity

I love it when my children come home from school and share what they've learned. Most of the time they share things that I already know. I am, after all, much older than them and fairly well-educated. But sometimes I learn something new and, in many cases, mind blowing. I've learned so much about space that I could now teach a short webinar on it!

The coolest thing I've ever learned from my kids is that the color of fall leaves is their natural color. The reason leaves are green in the spring and summer is because of all the chlorophyll in them.

Here's a fun little fact about me. I don't like fall. Ok, ok, you can stop with your shock and awe right now. I know it makes me a little strange. But fall has always made me sad. I am a spring lover—when everything comes back to life! In the fall Everything. Is. Dying.

And it hurts my heart to watch everything die.

Nonetheless, I was so fascinated by this little tidbit of knowledge that I dug in and did a little research—I had to know more! Here's what the website "Gardening Know How" says about the natural color of leaves:

> "Leaves are naturally orange and yellow. The green just normally covers this up. As the chlorophyll stops flowing, the tree starts to produce anthocyanin. This replaces the chlorophyll and is red colored. So, depending at which point in the fall leaf life cycle the tree is in, the tree will have green, yellow or orange leaves, then red autumn leaf color. Some trees produce anthocyanin faster than others, meaning that some trees skip right over the yellow and orange color stage and go straight into the red leaf stage. Either way, you end up with a brilliant display of leaves changing color in the fall."[2]

To take it a step further I visited NOAA (National Oceanic and Atmospheric Administration) to get some truly scientific answers.

"Weather factors such as temperature, sunlight, precipitation and soil moisture influence fall color arrival, duration and vibrancy. According to the United States National Arboretum, a wet growing season followed by a dry autumn filled with sunny days and cool, frostless nights results in the brightest palette of fall colors. Changes in weather can speed up, slow down or change the arrival time of fall's colorful foliage."[3]

In one specific NOAA article I read, the headline really caught my attention. "True colors come from the inside."

I don't know about you but this feels like a truly fantastic thing to learn and I couldn't believe I'd gone my entire life without this knowledge.

And then I started to think about nature in general and, specifically, the nature of human life. "The trees," I thought to myself, "become the truest version of themselves as they stop depending on an outside source to fuel them and are nearing the end of their lives. They are becoming the truest, most authentic and vulnerable versions of themselves—and it's breathtakingly brilliant."

Always one to go down a rabbit hole of learning, I knew I had to go even deeper. If trees behave this way, do other living things do it also? Is this something humans experience as well? Fortunately I had just the right source to go to for this question.

Back in December of 2018 I had the privilege of interviewing a woman named Alua Arthur for *The Brave Files* podcast. Alua is a Death Doula that has started to get some, much deserved, nationwide attention for her work.

I was, as you may be now, *very* curious about what a Death Doula was. And, I thought, this must be the saddest work possible!

But after my conversation with Alua on the podcast, I realized that there is so much grace and beauty in death. It is, in fact, as Alua says in the interview, "the only thing we can ever know for sure. We *will* die."

So as this little bit of knowledge about trees started taking root in my mind I asked Alua about it. Did she see a correlation between the natural phenomenon of leaves and the end of human life? Once again, this kind hearted, stunningly beautiful woman knew just what to say to make the natural flow of life feel magical and beautiful rather than like a sad ending.

"As a flower smells strongest at the end of life and leaves turn magnificent colors just before they fall, humans have the capacity to become our fullest, richest, most pungent selves just before death. We must choose to not let the fear of impending death impede us at our most ripe time."

We must choose, Alua said. And so, it seems, we must. Because we *will* die and, we *will* become the truest version of ourselves in that process, and in choosing to allow that authenticity to shine we are experiencing our bravest moment.

But then I began to wonder, does it *have* to be like this? How is it that we, as a species, are so advanced in some ways and so unadvanced in the ways of being the best possible version of ourselves? Is there a way to show up in the world with honesty, integrity and truth—right now? At this moment, rather than waiting for death?

For me, the answer is an emphatic yes. I call it being "radically authentic." And it's at the heart of The BRAVE Method because I don't believe you can actually practice and succeed with The BRAVE Method unless you embrace the concept of being radically authentic.

The BRAVE Method calls upon you to look at yourself and your life from the most honest lens possible. To set boundaries, sit in your mistakes and lessons, admit fault, ask for help, and do the hard work. Nothing is more radically authentic than that.

True Colors

I have a close knit family. My Granny (my Mom's mom) was only thirty five when I was born and although I always adored her, I didn't always agree with her. In fact, I would say I most often didn't agree with her on most major issues. She was riddled with faults—like the rest of us. But I loved her hard and I always knew that she loved me. She didn't have to tell me she loved me because it was apparent in her behavior, in the fact that she showed up for me. Always and in all ways as I was growing up. I didn't appreciate it the way I should have, the way I *wish I had*, when I was younger. This is a regret I'll always have but it's one I think many young people face. Life seems so full that we often overlook something as seemingly simple as a grandparent.

I knew growing up that my Granny and I were on different ends of the moral compass on things like racism and homophobia. I've been active in anti-racism work since before I knew it was a thing and never afraid to speak the truth or butt heads. But even with my strong will and loud mouth, coming out to my Granny was going to be one of the hardest things I ever did in my life.

When it became abundantly clear that I *had* to come out to her, because the rest of my family knew and it was time, I felt so much dread. In fact, my mother wanted to be the one to tell her. I'm not exactly sure why, perhaps in an effort to protect me from any emotional harm she anticipated I would experience, or if it was to control the narrative. In either case, it doesn't matter because my Granny wasn't having it. She wanted to hear the truth from me and she wasn't going to rest until she did.

I remember that phone call so well. Seeing her number come up on caller ID. That familiar feeling of heat rising up in my neck. The bile collecting in my throat. But this was the moment of truth and it was time to step into my brave in this situation. So I answered the phone. She asked me what I had to tell her and I spit it out pretty quickly. I'd practiced my coming out story plenty of times at this point so I was well prepared, if terrified. But by the grace of having never lived her own "perfect" life my Granny was kind and loving through the conversation. In the end, all she really said was, "You're mine, and I love you. Always."

Granny was kind and welcoming to my partner when they were introduced but she mostly kept her words and thoughts to herself on the matter of my gayness. Of course, I never asked her about it. I was too relieved and happy living my truth to care what she was thinking. And yet, there was this nagging sensation in my heart that she was disappointed in me. That I had let her down by being a lesbian.

And then she got sick. Remember when I said Granny was only thirty five when I was born? She was too young to be so sick she was dying. I wasn't prepared and it seemed so unfair. I also knew she didn't want to die. She wasn't ready, but life does what it wants and the only control we have over it is how we move through it. As the weeks turned into months it became more and more apparent that Granny wasn't going to survive her illness. She was a tiny shell of the powerhouse, attention demanding woman she'd always been. I did my best to call weekly and check in on her. We didn't talk long because I knew it took a lot out of her, but I wanted her to know I loved her and was there for her.

The last conversation I ever had with my Granny went like this:

Me: How are you feeling?

Granny: Oh, you know, not so great. But it's ok. Your mom's here taking care of me.

Me: That's good. I'm sorry I can't be there. You know how much I love you, right?

Granny: Yes honey, I know how much you love me.

Me: Ok, well, I know you're tired. I won't keep you any longer. Be sure to get lots of rest.

Granny: Heather ...

Me: Yes?

Granny: I hope you know how proud I am of you. What you did couldn't have been easy. You're the strongest person I know and I am so very proud of you. You are so brave.

Through my tears, I thanked her. By doing the honest, hard thing and showing up in the world with radical authenticity I had made her PROUD.

She was gone a week later.

I often wish I'd had more time with that version of Granny. Or maybe I wish I'd had more time with her knowing she was not, in fact, disappointed in me but, rather, proud of me. If only I'd trusted *myself* enough to have a conversation like this earlier, perhaps we could have spent more time in honesty, laughter, and relaxed joy together.

Granny was like the fall leaves in the end, brilliant, bold, beautiful. She no longer cared what the world told her to care about. She cared only about what was in her heart. And that heart centeredness allowed her to give me the best gift I had ever received. The best gift I *could* ever receive.

There's always more work to be done when it comes to radical authenticity. It's something we have to work hard, every day, to embody. But you have everything you need, inside of you, to let your true colors shine through. And, trust me, the world will bask in your beautiful brilliance.

TRISH

Brave Spotlight

* Changing the Rules and Creating Your Own Path

I first met Trish King in a writing program and I knew instantly that she was a special human. I couldn't help but seek her out for friendship. Trish had dedicated her entire life to serving in the military. She describes her job as an Infantryman as what you think of when little kids play "army." But Trish isn't just any Infantryman—she's America's first Transgender Infantryman and, subsequently, she was the first woman in active duty in the role. Now retired, Trish has been on the front lines many times. Not just in active duty but also as she neared retirement and beyond.

After fifteen long and dedicated years, Trish finally decided she was no longer willing to live a lie. It was time to admit her gender dysphoria and become, on the outside, the person she has always been on the inside. While she had wonderful support from her direct superiors, Trish came out and transitioned just before the metaphorical rug was pulled out from under transgender service members.

Prior to 2016 women weren't allowed to serve in combat-specific jobs. Trish has never taken this honor for granted and she continues to fight for freedom, truth and acceptance through her work in law making, non-profit support and by being an active participant on the Hill fighting for transgender rights.

Trish knows her role as an advocate is vital to the continued fight for social justice. For that reason, after retiring, she moved to Washington D.C. and continues discussions with Congress members and those with the ability to make meaningful changes in the

U.S. Government. This type of commitment to advocacy truly sends ripples through our communities. The call to action is clear: We all need to work together towards change.

Throughout my interview with Trish on *The Brave Files* podcast, I was reminded that there's real value in paying attention to the difference you're making. Don't just brush your achievements under the rug—embrace them! Others are watching and it's powerful to make a change for those who cannot do so themselves. She also reminds us to be realistic about our goals. Being radically authentic is a marathon, not a sprint. Some days are up, others are down. But stay the course and you'll get there.

These are the gifts of radical authenticity. The ability to stay loud and brave. To be active and aware with your eyes open. Radical authenticity allows you to be part of the solution, no matter what the problem. *

PART THREE

Keep the Momentum

Celebration and Gratitude

Growing Gratitude

Making the Brave Leap!

Now you know the details of The BRAVE Method. You're aware of some nastiness that can be lurking in the dark corners of your mind and you're ready to get started. That's awesome, by the way. I celebrate you and your commitment to making the brave leap! But I don't want you to forget about bringing light, love, joy, and happiness into it all. Without those things, why are we bothering in the first place?

Celebration and Gratitude

You know how you feel when you've completed something important, had a hard conversation, advocated for yourself, nailed a client meeting, or finished up a big project? That feeling of excitement and pride? That is a powerful feeling, one that helps you stay charged and ready to move on to the next big thing. That is a feeling that should always be celebrated.

Through my work, research, and study, I *know* that celebrating success is the key to motivation and even bigger successes. Aaron Anastasi, the author of *The Voice of Your Dreams* and *Your Prosperous Mind,* once told me that celebration is a lost discipline. I think he's right. There is something magical about the art of celebration. To truly celebrate all of your wins, personally and professionally, and not discredit the small ones, takes a lot of discipline. It also reaps the biggest rewards.

Imagine having that feeling I mentioned above woven through your life on a daily basis. Picture it, if you will: You feel awesome way more than you feel overwhelmed. There is always something to celebrate (Because there *really is* always something to celebrate).

One of the ways I tap into all of the amazing elements worth celebrating is through a gratitude ritual. I spend a few minutes each day writing down all of the things I am grateful for that day. Today, for example, I am already grateful that I managed to get my kids off to school on time (no easy feat with four kids and three schools), that I have a hot cup of coffee, and that I'm sitting down to work on this book at exactly the time I intended to. This isn't actually the norm, so on the days where the schedule goes off as intended I feel extreme gratitude! I'm also grateful for the clients I will serve today and the podcast interview I'm about to give. Taking the time to acknowledge gratitude gives me reason to celebrate. It instills a level of pride that I may otherwise lack. I even celebrate these wins with my accountability partners! I make every effort to bring celebration into as many aspects of my life as possible.

Each of us defines success differently. I truly believe that for me, success is found in even the smallest of achievements. I've discovered that to create the work-life balance I desire, I must celebrate every success, even if it seems inconsequential. Huge, fantastic leaps are wonderful, but never forget that it takes many small steps to achieve those larger goals. Don't forget about them along the way; they are the stepping stones that get you where you want to go.

I also love to celebrate my success with rewards. I am a big fan of rewards—Just ask my clients! That sounds exciting, doesn't it? Here are just a few ways I celebrate by rewarding myself (Notice that they range from tiny rewards to really big ones!):

- Take a walk when I have accomplished a task

- Ring a bell when I sign a new client
- Splurge on a specialty coffee from the local coffee shop
- Schedule a co-working day with some of my creative friends
- Allow myself a few minutes to browse through Facebook
- Get a pedicure
- Spirit one of my daughters away from school for a one-on-one lunch
- Buy theater or concert tickets
- Treat myself to a vacation

Because we all have days where we're super productive and days where achieving a small task feels like a major win, I encourage you to give each success its due celebration. *Success is success, even if it looks different today than it did yesterday and all wins count!*

Celebration Creates Gratitude

Life feels like it's on the fast train most of the time and that means we rarely stop to acknowledge our successes and wins. This is especially true with small wins. It's as if we're constantly moving the goalposts—So focused on what's next that we don't appreciate what's now. This results in feeling overwhelmed, behind, unsuccessful, unhappy, and as if we're never quite achieving "enough." I'm a big fan of setting and achieving goals, but for goodness sake, stop and smell the roses every once in a while!

TAKE A MOMENT TO CELEBRATE—
YOU'RE DOING A GREAT JOB!

When, after months of hard work, I sent my first book, *Shift Your Focus*, to the printer, I literally closed my computer, cranked up my favorite dance song (P!NK'S "Raise Your Glass"), and danced my heart out in my office. My partner sat there giggling at me, but she could feel my joy and relief. Was there more work to do? Of course. But for this moment, we both reveled in the fact that I had done the thing and it felt great. The joy associated with celebration is contagious!

The Difference Between Celebration and Gratitude

This is a solid question because the differences are subtle but important. It's best explained with examples.

Right now, I am sitting in my beautiful, sunlit office. I can feel the warmth of the sun through the windows and hear the birds chirping. I'm grateful—Grateful for the moment and taking the time to notice these natural wonders around me. There's gratitude for a moment's reflection and quiet.

Earlier today, I had a coaching call with a client who is starting to experience her own awakening. She is finding herself, her value, her voice, and her passions. When we hung up the phone, I knew I'd made a difference not only in her day, but her life. This was a win and it should be celebrated! You absolutely experience gratitude when you acknowledge and honor your wins, big and small.

Taking the time to acknowledge that for which you're grateful and to celebrate the small wins throughout your day, gives you more reason to celebrate. To smile quietly to yourself, have a dance party, reward yourself with a nice walk around the block, a hot cup of coffee, or a cold glass of champagne! Celebration can be anything you want. And it's the most beautiful, continuous circle!

When you're grateful, it causes internal celebration. When you celebrate, you're expressing a form of gratitude and so it goes—round and round. This is the perfect type of merry-go-round. Motion and movement that excites and motivates all of us. It's the type of ride that others see you taking and say, "I want some of that! How can I get on?" The partnership between gratitude and celebration is powerfully contagious.

The Red Plate

We have a specific plate in my house that we use for special occasions. It's a bright red plate and we call it, unsurprisingly, the Red Plate! The plate has the words "you are special today" written around it. And the idea is that after you use it, you write the special occasion in permanent marker on the back of the plate.

I received the Red Plate as a gift from my mother when I moved into my own home. It's something she had for me when I was growing up.

You might think that the Red Plate only gets used on someone's birthday, but it doesn't. The Red Plate gets used anytime there's something to celebrate! Because in my house, we celebrate everything, and we celebrate hard.

For me, celebration has always been about exuding joy in any way possible and as often as possible. And what I know for sure is that the more we celebrate with ourselves and with others, the more happiness and joy we are surrounded by. Celebration gives us pause to recognize things that are good and joyful and happy. And collective celebration brings people together in common joy.

I believe that celebration holds so much importance in our lives that I made it a regular part of *The Brave Files* podcast. I ask every guest I interview how they like to celebrate. And I get so many varied and wonderful answers from trips around the world, to ringing a bell when you make a sale, to dancing in your living room with your cat to Disney Princess music, to enjoying a piece of really delicious chocolate. Hearing how others pause to recognize and celebrate their wins helps us realize new and wonderful ways we can intentionally bring celebration into our own lives more fully.

PAIGE

Brave Spotlight

✳ Creating Joy and Changing Lives

Every year for my birthday, I fundraise for The Birthday Party Project (TBPP). The founder of the organization, Paige Chenault, is a friend of mine and a source of limitless inspiration. It seemed fitting to interview Paige for *The Brave Files* Podcast when it was due to air on my birthday!

TBPP is an amazing nonprofit organization that throws birthday parties for children living in shelters all over the United States. If you haven't heard of this life-changing organization, you're going to want to check them out. It's an understatement to say the world needs more people like Paige in it. She's constantly encouraging everyone she knows to live bigger and spread joy. This, she says, is how we change lives!

Paige was inspired to start the organization while planning her daughter's first birthday. As she was making grand plans, it occurred to her that many children would never have the opportunity to celebrate themselves. The thought broke her heart. Never one to back down from a challenge or an important project, she began building The Birthday Party Project.

Today, TBPP partners with shelters and transitional living facilities to throw birthday parties for the kids and families staying there. "Birthday Enthusiasts" (volunteers) give their time to throw the biggest monthly birthday bashes you can imagine. It takes an entire community to make these parties happen, so TBPP truly relies on the giving spirit of their diverse group of volunteers. It's through these volunteer efforts that we see just how much joy changes the lives of everyone involved. I've volunteered, along with my children, at several of these birthday parties and I can tell you they are extraordinarily wonderful to be a part of. It was also important for me to show my children that the world is wide and each person has a very different lived experience. I wanted them to stand up for all people, to love all people and to do their part in making a difference whenever they saw an opportunity to do so.

Every month, children celebrating their birthday receive a cake and presents. In addition, there are games and activities for all partygoers to enjoy. It's truly a gigantic celebration! Children receive the chance to simply be kids and experience joy, at least for this one hour a month. It's an overwhelmingly heartwarming experience for everyone involved.

Paige sees the impact of these birthday parties firsthand. Oftentimes, the guests of honor have never celebrated their birthday before. It may be their first time experiencing this level of attention or receiving so many warm wishes. The result of the celebration is often an obvious boost of confidence for the birthday children and their parents and even the other families in attendance.

Everyone who attends these celebrations can clearly see how children walk out of the room with their heads held high and their shoulders back. Obviously, this moment in time provides each child with a sense of community, love, respect, and a sense of worthiness. It infuses a little joy into their life circumstances. Imagine how you feel when you're celebrated. Now picture what that feeling could do for a child who is currently without a safe home to live in.

During the pandemic, Paige and the entire TBPP team worked tirelessly to bring these celebrations to children despite not being able to celebrate in person. The organization reinvented itself and got extremely creative. And as a result they have received support and endorsements from companies like Toyota, Southwest Airlines, Target, Frito Lays, and American Greetings. It just goes to show that when kindness and love are at the center of your motivation, nothing is impossible.

TBPP creates ripples of joy throughout the communities they touch. After each party, all over the country, morale at the agencies is boosted. A sense of community within each of the shelters or organizations increases too. Additionally, the children who are celebrated are shown they are not alone—a profound moment in any child's life. The Birthday Party Project is changing the world one joyful celebration at a time. Just like its founder, Paige. ✳

Joy Shared is Happiness Returned

When you have been blessed, the act of sharing that blessing with others makes it infectious. If you've busted your ass to create something awesome, sharing it with others has the potential to inspire them and encourage them.

Have you ever noticed how hard it is to be mad at someone who walks around happy all the time? You might get annoyed, right? You might think, "How can this person always be so happy?" But you still cannot help but have a slightly elevated mood when you're around them.

This is where mindset can make all the difference. I have a screen saver on my phone that says "Choose Happiness." Not because I am always happy but because it is my daily goal— to find the joy inside my every day and to be as infectious with it as possible.

But nothing makes joy more powerful than sharing it. The happiness that returns to you is the greatest feeling ever. That's one of the reasons I love The Birthday Party Project so much and partnered my Chaos to Clarity course with them. The work they do— bringing celebration and joy into the lives of children who have so little—is pure magic. And I have seen this magic work on the volunteers as well as the kids.

Find something you love, do that thing, and then share it with others. If the thing you love isn't your work, that is perfectly fine. Seek this joy in every corner of your life. What lights you up? What makes you feel connected? Do that thing and don't let anything or anyone stand in your way. Then shout it from the rooftops.

BRAVE Action

Celebration

What are you celebrating today?

Take this opportunity to list out five wins from your day. Even if it's hard, trust me, you can always find the wins if you're looking for them. Sometimes my wins are getting out of bed and taking a shower! On those days, it's especially important to give myself props for showing up and not giving up.

Who can you share these wins with? Spread the love and bring community into your celebrations. I promise it will make them even more wonderful.

How are you going to celebrate?

Celebrate these things together and then see what type of magic appears.

Growing Gratitude

We've all been there. We've all woken up on the wrong side of the bed, gotten extremely pissed off when someone cut in front of us in line, or while waiting at a stoplight. There are a million things each day that can make us angry. But what happens when we allow those little things to take up precious time and space in our lives and our minds?

Well, thoughts become things, folks. So if you focus on all the icky things, you're going to come up with nothing but more icky things.

What's the big idea? Gratitude.

If you want to feel better, happier, and be more successful than you've ever thought possible, develop a consistent gratitude practice! Yep, that's right. Developing a practice that regularly invites gratitude into your life helps you focus on the gifts and blessings that constantly surround you. It crowds out the negative thoughts and keeps positivity in the forefront of your mind.

Our brains cannot hold both negative and positive thoughts at once. While life will always be messy, there's a lot of joy to be found even among the ups and downs. When we feel joyous, everything we touch is better. You can turn negatives into positives. Trust me, I've been there.

After a decade of marriage and four kids, I came out. Yes, of the closet. And it was hard. Coming out eventually led to divorce— Because staying married to the wrong gender isn't good for anyone, but goodness, did it suck! A couple of short years after that, I closed the luxury wedding planning business I'd owned for nearly twenty years. Those were two of the most difficult and painful experiences of my life. They were also a core element of my perceived sense of self. It was hard—Really hard. But on the other side of that pain was...me. That's right, I was on the other side. The real me. The authentic, take the world by storm, take-no-bullshit ME! I've since built a thriving coaching practice. I speak on international stages, I'm a published author (and fabulous you is reading my book right this minute!), and I host a super kick-ass podcast. I'm crushing this life thing—Finally. Every day isn't perfect and neither am I. But there's never a moment where I feel like I'm letting myself down because I'm showing up as authentically as possible.

Building this life was intentional and I couldn't have done it without gratitude. I learned about gratitude, studied it, and put hard work into making it a daily practice. It's now so ingrained in me that my natural response is to turn something negative into a positive on a dime. It wasn't always like that, but I'm sure glad it is now! The queen, Oprah, said it best in her bestselling Memoir *What I Know For Sure*[1] ·

"Being grateful all the time isn't easy. But it's when you least feel thankful that you are most in need of what gratitude can give you: perspective. Gratitude can transform any situation. It alters your vibration, moving you from negative energy to positive. It's the quickest, easiest, most powerful way to effect change in your life. This I know for sure." - **Oprah Winfrey**

I depend heavily on my daily gratitude practice. I've learned to rely on gratitude when things get difficult. It's come to be my safe space, my home base. No matter what, I always know that if I look for it, there's something to be grateful for in each and every situation life throws at me. That certainly doesn't mean it always comes easily—not even close. There are days when my list is short. At times, I struggle to come up with anything other than the absolute basics: Health, family, and friends. But I work to dig into those basics and be specific. It's an excellent opportunity to remind myself of how good things actually are. The next few chapters will explain *why* I love gratitude so much.

Gratitude is Grounding

When I first started practicing gratitude, I'd list out my five things at night before bed and quickly found myself actively reframing my day. Some days were easier than others! There were days where I signed new clients, booked speaking engagements, or was a guest on a podcast. Those days the gratitude came flooding out. But at other times, like nights where my kids were having a hard time sleeping or I wasn't sure when the next client was going to book—ahem, how the bills were going to get paid—I was essentially forced to find the good things deep within the not-so-good things.

I began to be grateful for the forced reframe. If you have kids, you know that sleeping sandwiched between them is the single most uncomfortable way to sleep *ever*. But as I laid in bed between my daughters, then four and eight years old, I would look at their peaceful sleeping faces and remind myself that they wouldn't be little for long. They wouldn't need me to comfort them at night forever. The growing pains we experience with young children, as with young businesses, are all short-lived. In that moment I would be so grateful for the opportunity to give them peace and comfort. To feel their tiny, soft hands wrapped around mine. I learned to just inhale it and not wish it away.

The same could be said for business. As an entrepreneur, it is often feast or famine and the famine can play powerful tricks on your mind.

"Am I good enough?"

"Do people want what I have to offer?"

"Is anyone out there paying attention!?"

Because of my gratitude practice, I put myself in a position to look past those fears and find the successes. If I wasn't completely booked out then I had more time for writing, something I love doing and wish I had more time for. When my schedule wasn't jam packed I could check a few things off the "I would like to do this but never have the time" list. I learned that there is always a way to feel successful and proud of what you have accomplished, even if it is not in the manner you originally intended.

Gratitude Can Change Your Mindset

My mindset shifted completely when I went all in on gratitude. When frustrating or difficult things appear, I find myself instantly looking for the "bright side" so that I can list it in my evening gratitude entry. Being grateful means I'm not allowing myself to go completely down the rabbit hole when things go south. While this was difficult at first, eventually it became second nature. That "reframe" is an extraordinary gift.

Now I even find myself tapping into gratitude in situations that make me angry! When I'm driving and the traffic is super slow, or when my kids are screaming at each other, or when a client is past due on a payment, I've learned to stop the internal bitching and instead say something I am grateful for. In these situations, anything works. The trick is simply to stop focusing on the negative thing and start focusing on the positive one.

I also learned that some days are just so bad that my daily gratitude felt like a really big stretch. I remember one night the best I could come up with is "I am glad I woke up" and "I am glad I have working legs." But, and this is the funny thing about gratitude, I later realized that wasn't much of a stretch at all. I am really, really grateful to wake up each day and have working legs. There are many others who don't have those gifts. On a terrible, horrible, no good, very bad day, the simple reminder that it is truly not that bad is such a blessing.

This doesn't mean you can't have off moments or days. You can and you will. You deserve to feel all of your feelings, roll around in them even. Be super honest about those feelings! It's okay to bitch and feel shitty sometimes. It's completely normal to do so. The real key is in *choosing* not to stay in that space for too long.

Gratitude Taught Me About Forgiveness

Forgiveness is a gift we give ourselves. It's rarely about the person or people we're forgiving. It gives us freedom from something that has taken up residence in our hearts and minds far longer than it deserves to. It opens up space for really wonderful things to happen.

As I continue to tap deeper and deeper into my gratitude experience, I find myself far more willing to forgive others, and myself. Mostly, I decided that this shit wasn't worth holding onto and it wasn't worth missing out on wonderful things to hold grudges or be angry.

I also learned to forgive myself far more quickly. On days where I feel like I can't do enough or be enough, I use my gratitude as a way of acknowledging my humanity. I'm grateful for surviving, for giving myself grace. I can chalk it up to a crappy day and start over tomorrow.

Gratitude motivates me.

What I love most about gratitude is that there are truly no limits. A grateful heart is a grateful heart—no matter what fills that heart up. A gratitude practice is whatever you make it. Gratitude has the power to serve as a serious motivation in your life. Use it to continue pushing through. Focusing on the positive will give you a much-needed boost when you're feeling drained and frustrated.

Gratitude Causes Physical Changes!

The physical effects of daily gratitude include better sleep and a stronger immune system. Feeling calmer, in control, and happier are added bonuses. It's even been proven that having a regular gratitude practice lowers your risk of heart disease.

Here's what one article from Harvard Medical School had to say about gratitude:

"Many studies show that people prone to negative emotions have a higher risk of heart disease. Negative emotions are associated with the release of stress hormones and a physical stress response, resulting in a higher heart rate and blood pressure.

Scientists hypothesize that positive people who have a 'glass half-full' approach to life are less likely to experience this stress response. Basically, those who tend to look for the bright side of negative situations can avoid the damage that stress inflicts on the cardiovascular system. Another hypothesis is that people with a positive outlook are more likely to use healthy coping strategies like problem-solving to overcome obstacles and manage stressors, whereas people with a negative outlook tend toward unhealthy coping strategies like self-medicating with food and other substances."[2]

Gratitude is the Pathway to Deep Happiness

Gratitude brings peace and contentment. When you take the time to focus on the good in your life, no matter how small, your eyes will open to other goodness around you. Basically, gratitude has a snowball effect. The more you express it, the more you see it. The more you see it, the more awe-inspiring emotion you will experience. The idea is simple. Gratitude quite literally changes lives.

I've said before that "Joy shared is happiness returned." Expressing and sharing gratitude has the same powerful effect! Your gratitude can change someone else's life, too!

The impact of outwardly expressed gratitude is oftentimes unbelievable. It can make *that* big of a difference! When we share our joys with others, they are invited to celebrate alongside us. Through sharing in joy, they are inevitably encompassed by a powerful force that transcends our day-to-day lives. Living in a space of gratefulness elevates our moods and has direct power to change our perception of the world around us.

I enjoy hearing what other people are grateful for so much that I am in a Facebook group specifically for expressing gratitude. I've created several episodes of *The Brave Files* podcast dedicated to it as well, and I strongly encourage you to go listen to them right now (they are listed in the back of the book). I promise these episodes will fill you with all sorts of wonderful feelings and provide a little connection, motivation, and inspiration along the way.

I fully understand that some days and situations suck. It's silly to believe we will never have negative emotions. The real magic in reaching down deep for gratitude is the ability to shut the negative emotions down and not let them own you.

Here are a few situations in which you may feel hopeless but looking for gratitude can cause a deep impact:

- You have a flat tire. This is a real bitch. No one has time for this. Be grateful that you did not get into an accident with a blown tire.

- You got in an argument with a dear friend. This feels bad. None of us want to hurt or be hurt by someone we care about. Be grateful that you are capable of feeling deep emotions and that you have someone in your life that is special enough to want to fix the situation.

- You are stuck in a serious traffic jam from a car accident. This one gets me every time. I have places to go and people to see and kids to parent and this frustrates me. Then I remember that I could have been in the car accident. I am so grateful to be stuck in traffic and not in the ambulance. I will get to go home and hug my kids.

It may take time.

If you are new to practicing gratitude, cut yourself some slack. It takes time to build strong habits. A new practice doesn't immediately take hold. First, you have to begin with a plan; Put a system for tracking your gratitude and specific goals in place. I am a big fan of gratitude journaling (or creating lists) and I have almost all of my clients begin this practice as well. Writing down things that you're most grateful for changes something in your brain; when you change your brain, you change your life. And now we know there is serious science behind this!

When you practice gratitude, you aren't just thinking about feeling grateful; You are physically logging it. Scheduling time every single day to think about and acknowledge that which you are most grateful for is the first step to success. And you know how I feel about a schedule—time block the hell out of that gratitude!

> *"We can't change anyone but ourselves, but when we change ourselves, the people around us change!"*

Finally, if you practice gratitude and celebrate joy with others, everyone will be changed. Your energy levels will skyrocket; Your drive to push through will increase. Gratitude keeps us moving when the going gets tough. It will carry you through times of challenge and heartache and give you much-needed perspective. It will even motivate you through blocks in your business. A simple change in mindset can alter the entire way you and those around you look at the world.

Gratitude is the key to success.

All you need to do is express it.

Create a Habit of Gratitude

You may be wondering, when it comes to gratitude as a whole, just how far are you supposed to take it? The answer is simple: As far as you'd like! The more you create a habit of gratitude in your life, the easier it will come to you. I've experienced this firsthand. Just as it is with any other habit, creating the routine takes work. Once it's part of your daily ritual, however, I promise you'll see a shift. Your brain is trainable.

Training your brain to rely on gratitude will completely transform your life! Partner gratitude with a well-laid plan and you've got a winning combination.

Be sure to share your gratitude

In my opinion, sharing gratitude makes a gigantic difference. It's one thing to acknowledge all that you have, experience, and feel. It's another thing entirely to express that gratitude outwardly. When you share your gratitude with the people around you, it encourages others to do the same.

You don't have to believe it to try it

I know some of you may not fully buy into the idea that expressing gratitude can be life-changing. That's ok. I'm also guessing you can't find a single reason why one should *not* strive to be grateful. I smile as I type this because I often talk with clients about trying something they're not really sure will work. I always urge them to just *do it*, whether they think it'll work or not. We should make way more effort to try things without knowing what the end result will be in general. And guess what, when clients try a consistent gratitude practice, it works! So long as they're consistent in the effort, it fucking works.

You see, no matter what you believe, nothing negative can come from gratitude. There really is no risk at all in giving it a try. It's a lot like kindness. Both kindness and gratitude bring people together, and they both have a real impact.

AMY

BRAVE Spotlight

✳ Check Your Comfort Zone at the Door

Meet Amy, a self-proclaimed middle-aged service addict. Amy was once a public interest attorney, but as she approached her 50th birthday she felt a little stuck in her life. She was called to do something momentous, to experience something truly unique to mark the occasion. These ideas finally came together as her innovative platform "Follow Me to 50." The project took her out of her comfort zone and helped her discover a new passion—*herself!* When I interviewed her for *The Brave Files* podcast, Amy told me this deep look inside herself offered countless opportunities to be grateful for all she was experiencing. And if she hadn't taken the time to listen to her intuition and start "Follow Me to 50," she may well have missed it all!

For the "Follow Me to 50" project, Amy decided to do three major challenging things that mattered to her.

- Dedicate herself to public service by doing fifty solo public service projects

- Start her own blog

- Do a fifty mile walk

It was important to Amy that she complete each of these tasks alone. This was an experience with herself and for herself. It's wonderful to share experiences with others, but Amy knew that if she brought family or friends along for the ride, she wouldn't be able to keep the focus specifically on herself and she wouldn't enjoy the experience as thoroughly.

Although she was beyond scared, Amy told herself she was ready. It was time to take the plunge. She threw herself fully into the activities with enthusiam.

Amy had no idea how to write a blog but gave it a go in order to publicly chronicle her journey. She pushed herself and journaled all of her experiences. The blog was a wonderful resource for holding herself accountable and to document and share her experience.

These days, Amy encourages others to do what she did; to find purpose and passion at every stage in life and to expand the traditional notions of community to inspire actionable interaction. The highlight of Amy's work is teaching others to invest in their communities and themselves, as well as to appreciate all that comes with these gifts.

During our interview, I learned how her journey really started and how she overcame many of the obstacles blocking her way.

Public service was in her blood, so to speak. Despite being an ambitious woman for most of her life, her goals didn't reach beyond getting her law degree, getting married, and having kids. Yet it became clear as she approached fifty that these things were no longer enough and she'd lost herself in the process of doing everything right.

Finally, after three decades of putting others first and watching those around her find passion in their work, Amy decided it was time to put herself first and priortize nourishing herself. It was time to honor and celebrate herself and the gifts *she* brought to the world.

Amy has realized the blessing of solitude and how it can help people find themselves even as they withdraw from the crowd. She now uses her blog to inspire others on their journey to finding purpose and passion. ✳

When Things Get Hard, Focus on Gratitude

I've participated in National Novel Writing Month (NaNoWriMo) for three years in a row. Each year is a completely different experience. The first year, I wrote every day for 23 and then, when Thanksgiving hit, I traveled to see family and I just wasn't able to prioritize the writing time as I had hoped. I'd written 27,000 words at that point—Just over half of the NaNoWriMo goal of 50,000 words. I didn't spend a lot of time beating myself up for "not finishing" because it was the first time in my life that I'd written 23 days in a row and I was extremely proud of that accomplishment. I decided to allow that to be a win and to be grateful for the lessons and gifts of my first NaNoWriMo experience.

For the second year, I decided to make a solid plan (You know how much I love systems and planning!) to write every day and hit that 50,000 word goal. Here's what my plan looked like:

- Three mornings a week I would get up at 6:00 am (this may not be early for some of you but it's super early for this night owl) and write for an hour.

- Once a week, I'd meet up with a group of local writers also participating in the program and write together for two hours. (You always need extra time when there's chit chat involved).

- The other three days a week, I schedule an hour of writing in my daily work schedule.

It was a solid plan, but here's the thing…

Sometimes shit happens. I had to be flexible and willing to change plans, if necessary. What was non-negotiable was writing. Every. Damn. Day. So if my writing time needed to shift, so be it. I didn't go to bed until I had written at least 1600 words every damn day. I'd made this commitment to myself and no one was holding me accountable for it but me. I refused to let myself down! And I didn't! I completed my book in LaGuardia Airport, flying home after spending Thanksgiving with my partner and her family. I remember bursting into tears in the middle of the airport. Pride. Relief. Gratitude. I felt all the emotions as I typed the final words and closed my computer. I celebrated by doing a Facebook Live and sharing my accomplishment. I was so damn proud!

And then there was NaNoWriMo 2020, the third year I planned to participate. I knew I would write the book in your hands right now. I'd outlined it months earlier and I desperately wanted to follow the same plan I'd used in year two, but it was 2020. We were in the middle of a pandemic. My kids were remote learning. I knew I'd be deluding myself to think there would be time to write every day.

I had a choice to make. I could either attempt to follow the previous year's plan and, most likely, fail. Or I could make a new plan. This year was different because unlike previous years, I had every intention of publishing this book. And I didn't want to make it harder than it needed to be or let myself and my future readers (YOU!) down.

So I decided to get really, really honest with myself. If I couldn't write every day, what could I do to be successful in this endeavor?

Eventually I realized that I needed to write on the days my kids were not with me. Trust me, friends, there's a silver lining in all situations, even the ones that feel crappy. Because I have shared custody of my kids, they are with their other parent half of the time. So I had fifteen days to write this book rather than thirty.

That meant over 3200 words per writing day. No excuses. Some days it was extremely difficult. Some days I didn't write as many words as I wanted. Life—pandemic life at that—had its claws in me! I had clients to serve, a podcast to produce, a family to care for, and my own mental health to maintain (The pandemic took a serious toll on me emotionally—as it did for many of you, I'm sure).

In the end I decided to spend the last weekend of the month alone in a hotel room, writing. My only objective was to finish this book. And guess what, I did it! Although these are not the last pages of the book you'll be reading (thanks to an amazing editing team) they are the last pages I wrote. Alone, in my hotel room, grateful as hell.

You may be wondering why I'm sharing all of this with you and why it's listed under the gratitude section. So let me tell you. This is hard work. And I've learned that when things get hard, gratitude is what gets me through.

While writing this book, my list of things to be grateful for is plentiful. Allow me to share just some of my gratitude with you:

- I found time to write despite supporting remote learners

- We all stayed healthy and none of us contracted COVID-19

- I had virtual writing buddies to encourage and support me

- My partner always encouraged me and never gave me any grief over time dedicated to writing outside my normal work hours

- I had the financial means to stay in a hotel room for two nights to complete this manuscript

- I had an abundance of chocolate available when writing got rough

- I had the admiration and support of my entire community of BRAVEHearts (my nickname for my clients and folks I support through the Brave on Purpose Community and those who regularly listen to *The Brave Files* podcast) who are eager to read this book and encouraged me to stay the course

Never forget that when things get rough, gratitude can be your partner and help you pull through.

Brave Action

Gratitude

Creating a dedicated gratitude practice takes time, but it's worth it.

First, set aside a specific time each day to record what you're grateful for and why. Be specific and intentional about this. For example, some of my clients record their gratitude before bed each night. Others like to do it in the morning as a reflection on the previous day.

I like to do it in the evenings as well. It makes for a nice end cap to the day and allows me much-needed time for reflection and celebration.

Use these prompts to connect with gratitude on a deeper level (or go further and grab a copy of one of my Gratitude Journals).

Prompts:

- List five things you're grateful for and why. When doing this, resist the urge to pick the obvious, like your house, your family, your job. Be more specific. Look at gratitude from a micro level.

- Look around you and list five things you are grateful for that you can see or feel at this exact moment.

- Ask yourself how you expressed gratitude towards others and if there's a way to improve upon your outward expression of gratitude.

Eventually you will learn to take your gratitude practice even further. These advanced levels of gratitude can become second nature and are excellent ways to get out of a rut, think creatively and remind yourself what you're really working so hard for.

Having a well rounded and grounded gratitude practice is also helpful when you're going through the Three R's. Take a moment and list out something that you consider to be an epic failure in your life or perhaps something that was extremely painful. Now ask yourself, what goodness came from those things? Sit with that until you can list at least five positives from those negative experiences. Wash, rinse, and repeat as often as possible.

Making the Brave Leap!

Here are a few final thoughts on how to approach this brave leap and design a life and business that you love.

You're not lacking motivation. You may be searching for motivation, but that's not where you should be looking. No matter who you are or what your job is, consistent output is important. You might even say it's crucial to success. The challenge, however, is that it doesn't always come easy!

I wish someone would give me a dollar for every time I thought I lacked motivation. I'd be sitting on a beach with a cocktail and a personal chef! Like most people, I've spent a good period of my life thinking I was fighting for motivation. That "lack of motivation" was the root of my problems. But I've put a great deal of effort into managing and mastering my mindset. Through that work, I discovered the importance of finding sources of motivation. You see, it wasn't the motivation I was lacking—it was a source for the motivation.

When we are committing to something, anything really, it's crucial to understand why you want to do this thing or take that action. Tapping into the source and desire for completing said task or project is what provides motivation.

I want to produce valuable content for my readers, clients, conference attendees, and listeners. But why do I want to produce valuable content? It's not just to say I've done it. It's not for praise or completion. I want to produce the content because I know once it's out there, it can help people. If something I produce connects with just one person and gives them an idea or inspiration, then I'm doing my job. If what I produce allows someone to feel less alone or part of something greater, then I am doing my job. Providing relatable content is one of the aspects of my business that I love, and my clients and listeners deserve it.

So why the struggle to stay consistent?

It wasn't until I realized that motivation comes from within that I truly started to change my mindset. Sure, there are plenty of things you can do to kick start that feeling: listen to inspirational podcasts (Malcolm Gladwell's "Revisionist History" is one of my favorites), find a really great pump-up song (P!NK's "Raise Your Glass," anyone?), read a book that totally gets you jazzed (Shonda Rhimes' "Year of Yes" comes to mind)—but those things don't give you the motivation you need. You have to dig down deep and cultivate it within yourself.

Always ask yourself, "Why?"

If you are a parent you have, undoubtedly, listened to your children ask "But why?" over and over again until you want to scream and run away. Trust me, I've been there—but these kids are on to something. Wanting to truly and deeply understand why something needs to be done or not done is important. Connecting with the why of the matter changes everything it touches. It takes something from "I need to do this" to "I want to do this." It humanizes the desire and our motivation behind our actions.

One of the best examples I've ever seen of this was in P!NK's Amazon Documentary, "All I Know So Far." There's a specific scene where she's on her tour bus with her family, driving to a performance at Wembley Stadium. Her son (who I think was about two at the time) was asking question after question and she patiently answered them all. With each answer she gave, he responded with "Why?" Now I know how annoying that can be, especially if you're gearing up for something as big as performing at Wembley Stadium but what happened next took my breath away. The young boy says "Mama, are you going to sing there?" and he points to the stadium. "Yes," P!NK responds. "Why?" Her son asks. "Because singing makes people happy."[3]

Mic drop.

Prior to hearing her answer, I answered for her in my head. I expected an answer like, "Because it's my job." But no, that's not what she said. I mean, it *is* her job to perform, but that's not *why* she was performing. She performs because singing makes people happy, even herself—even when it's challenging or difficult.

When you know your why, the motivation shows up in ways you may never even expect.

Last week, I was on a coaching call with a client; he was telling me how he "really should" be making more sales calls. I get it. If you have something to sell, it's necessary to get out there and do the selling. But as Simon Sinek says, "People don't buy what you do; they buy why you do it."[4] Making a sales call without understanding what you want from that call, and why it's worth it, is an act of futile frustration.

Ask yourself this: What is the *want* behind everything I think I 'need' or 'should' do? What is the desired result you will achieve from having done the thing? That, my friend, is what will motivate you.

I suggest turning your wants into positive affirmations. These can be tools used on the path to motivation. Staying aware of your thoughts and mindset and intentionally using affirmations or language to remind you of why you are pushing through a difficult (or even boring) task can mean the difference between doing something or not. With constant repetition, these thoughts and mindsets become part of the universe and they manifest for you.

If you consistently work on your internal motivation, you will soon see changes in your everyday life. Like a muscle, your mind needs conditioning to grow.

Progress is Rarely Linear

Wouldn't it be nice if we could just dream something up, decide how we want to get it, and then have all of the puzzle pieces fall perfectly into place? It's a lovely little image, isn't it? But the reality is, our lives and businesses take many different twists and turns. Sometimes we never get to our big dream because the path changes along the way. Sometimes our dreams change along the way. Or maybe you didn't start with an "end dream." Perhaps you are only now discovering a destination you want to reach. The road to achieving your dreams is windy and progress is almost never linear.

Let that sink in for a minute. If you were to keep track of your life on a line graph, you would see many dips in the graph. If you're lucky, you might find a few major upticks. But what really matters is that there's overall forward movement.

When I look back on my life and think about where I expected to go as a college student, or when I was newly graduated, or when I first got married, the only thing that was consistent in those days was forward motion. I really didn't have any long term dreams beyond having a family. I didn't even know I could have other dreams. I just put my head down and did the thing. In those days, the graph looked pretty steady and that never seemed to bother me.

And then everything got shaken up.

Life threw me a serious curveball. As it turned out, keeping my head down and just doing the thing wasn't lighting me on fire. In fact, it was slowly killing me. I had nothing in common with my spouse. My babies were perfect but everything else in my life fell flat. If I had a graph to look back on, it would have shown a major plummet. Sometimes things have to get really bad before you wake up enough to say, "I need something different."

For me, that wake-up call happened in phases. It started with personal awareness of my deep unhappiness in my marriage and the realization that I had married the wrong gender (go ahead and giggle there; it's usually where I pause for laughs). Realizing halfway through my life that I was not the person I always thought I was shook things up like no other. Then I realized I had to tell other people about this realization, and that was terrifying. Sometimes we have to create the right situations out of the wrong ones.

> *"Sometimes we have to create the right*
> *situations out of the wrong ones."*

If you've had a similar realization that the life you always imagined isn't the life you were intended for, you have two choices:

Embrace who you are authentically or pretend nothing has changed. I chose to embrace myself because pretending was a whole hell of a lot harder to live with. I realize that sounds crazy. Completely turning my life upside down was hard—like, really, really hard! There was a lot at risk and it was unbelievably painful but the idea of never embracing my true self or reaching my true potential hurt much more.

Then I realized I needed and wanted more from my work—from myself. I wanted to make a bigger impact in the lives of others. I wanted to light people up, help them connect with their own authentic selves and then do something about it. I had a story to tell that had the power to inspire others. This is where we start to see the line graph make an uptick. Once you truly tap into your superpower and start listening to what the Universe has in store for you, things change shape. But it all starts by identifying your needs. How can you get somewhere if you don't know where you want to go?!

Let's be real with each other. Life is hard. Being an adult can be overwhelmingly hard. Being a corporate professional or an entrepreneur is hard. Being a good parent, partner, friend and community member is hard. Sometimes it's all just fucking hard!

I am a kick-ass Success Coach and CEO of a thriving business, but just like most entrepreneurs, I sometimes wonder how it will all continue to work out. Some months are freaking great and some I wonder how the bills will get paid. These days, I identify what makes my heart sing and what taps into who I want to be in the world, what I have to give, and why it really matters. I'm honest with myself if I need to let something go. Not all goals need to be met; there are plenty of times we need to let go of something good to usher in something great.

Progress is almost never linear. Don't be so hard on yourself.

Making Commitments

If you really want to accomplish something, make commitments. Be specific about them and then do the thing. Commitments involve declaring an intention and then taking action to follow through.

On the cusp of a new year, we seem to love change. Changes are good. You probably reflect on the past year, create some type of vision board and maybe even set a Word of The Year for yourself. I'm willing to bet you also set some goals. But here's a hard truth. Those goals are not likely to happen without some serious intention and planning behind them.

It's time to talk about making and keeping commitments. No matter how many times you journal, how awesome your systems are, or anything else you have put in place, none of us are actually productive or effective unless we make and keep commitments! The proof is in the pudding, folks!

Commitments are everything. *Everything!* We're talking about more than a to-do list. More than deliverables. Without commitments, it is impossible to achieve work-life balance and it is impossible to maintain productivity. It is impossible to have a successful business. The best laid plans fall to the wayside.

Something *really* important to point out here is that commitments are different from goals. Everyone knows the importance of setting goals. Goals are great. They are things you work towards, something you strive to do or achieve. And then there is making a commitment. Commitments are things you *will do*, not things you hope to one day do. Some commitments are things you are going to do, while some are ways you are going to be. During each of my workshops and coaching sessions, my clients commit to things that they *know* will create growth and change—Like sending a specific email or writing for at least fifteen minutes a day. Commitments come in many different forms and can be personal or professional. I have one client who commits to walking around her home, chanting a mantra that helps her feel empowered.

Commitments are more than a to-do list. They're the follow-through on the boundaries you previously set. Commitments give those boundaries intention. And nothing happens without intention!

A few months ago, a client mentioned that he was working all of the time, but was still unfocused and not getting enough done. I suggested he commit to keeping track of everything he did from the time he woke up until the time he went to bed. I wanted him to identify how and where he was spending his time. After tracking his hours for a week, we looked at what could be shifted or released so that he was more efficient. By the time we finished, he said it was like more hours magically appeared. The magic was in the commitment and the intention that went behind the work, choosing to be aware of time poorly spent and then creating a new plan—Because we all know there are only twenty four hours in a day and you need to sleep some of the time!

Often when working with clients I discover that their "way of being" in a situation is part of what's holding them back. A great example is constantly discrediting a win before announcing it. We've all done it: "Well, I didn't do as much as I could have, but I am proud of what I accomplished." Did you hear that? You've already said it's not good enough before we've even started.

Get creative with your commitments by *not limiting them to tasks.* Try committing to a specific mindset or "way of being" in a situation. One of my clients struggles to get out of her own way and just start. I have her chanting "Imperfect action is always better than no action. I don't have to know everything to start." The commitment here is to retrain her brain, give herself some grace, and just take any action, no matter how imperfect it might be. Commitments involve declaring an intention and then taking action to follow through.

One of my clients has an email issue. She admits that email has been her nemesis forever. When the emails come in, she might take a glance at them, but then she moves back into whatever she was doing before. This means they pile up and it is overwhelming as hell. Then, she committed to only looking at emails at specific times of the day. One she reviewed the emails, she was to take instant action on them. They were either sent to someone else to take care of, responded to, scheduled, filed or trashed!

When committing to a specific task, rather than a way of being, be sure to schedule them directly into your calendar. After each of my personal coaching sessions, I enter my commitments into my calendar so that they don't fall off my radar.

It's important to note that when it comes to "ways of being" and changing big habits, I strongly suggest you make them bite-sized chunks. Typically, I recommend committing to something for a week, checking in at the end of the week, and consciously deciding to recommit to that thing or let it go.

I believe it is *very* important to take action on something *right away.* So consider committing to just that. When you identify something that needs to be done or changed, build it into your schedule somehow to take immediate action.

When I work with clients 1:1 (or even in a group setting), I always ask them to make a firm commitment to the things they agree to do. It's how I end every single coaching session. If you are going to write a blog post, I want to know what day and time you intend to sit down and write. Then I want you to promptly go and schedule it in your calendar.

Why do I push for that level of intensity and commitment? Because without it, most things don't actually happen! Making and keeping commitments is hard. Without the dedicated intention behind it, things simply get lost in the shuffle! But the truth of the matter is that personal commitment and intention is where the magic lies.

Yes, commitment can be scary.

Just the other day, I had a client (who I have known for years) tell me she doesn't really "like" schedules. She feels tied down when she uses one. I giggled because I've heard this line before. It's what disorganized people tell themselves to justify why they are disorganized. They're "free spirits," they say. "A schedule will kill my soul."

But intentional commitments set you free. I say this without hesitation because I have seen it over and over again. While it isn't always easy, I can tell you that if you work on it consistently, commitment becomes a habit. So I encourage you to set an intention towards your goals and really go for it.

Okay...but how?

That's the next question! You may be ready to commit to the next phase of your life or business, but you have no idea what that actually looks like. It feels tricky. I've been there. As with all other changes, real commitment requires a game plan. So let's dive in together.

Step one: Start with one or two big commitments for the year.

This is not a to-do list. This is vision planning. Who do you want to be in the coming year? What do you want to experience, both as a person and a professional?

You owe it to yourself to take this seriously. Write your commitment down. Physically log it. In some cases you may even want to say it out loud. Let the Universe know it's your intention and then do the work. Trust me; it makes a difference.

Step two: Post your commitment in a central place.

Whether you keep a post-it note front and center on your desk or you write across a giant dry-erase board in your kitchen, make your commitment visible. I personally hang my commitments above my desk as a reminder of what I'm working towards.

This step will look different for everyone, but it's not a step you'll want to skip.

Step three: Break your commitment into smaller pieces or goals.

This part is really important! If you're going to succeed and really see your commitment stick, it's imperative you break it into small, manageable tasks or goals. These smaller items become your daily or weekly commitments.

I like to write down my intentions for the week. This includes the top three things I want to accomplish. Sometimes this all seems tedious, but it's crucial for this personal work. Growth stems from clarity, so you need to get crystal clear on *how* you will make these things happen. I've learned that if I don't write down what I'm focusing on, I tend to lose track and find myself wasting a lot of valuable time. There are so many distractions in our everyday lives, so keeping your boundaries at the forefront is key. You may be surprised at how much creativity can be unlocked with strong, healthy boundaries.

Once I identify each of the smaller commitments required to achieve a larger commitment or vision, I take an extra step and put these items in my schedule. In doing so, I create intentional time and space to complete each task. I am promising myself this will be undisturbed and dedicated time. In turn, I get my work done faster and more effectively, and I *really* like being fast and effective because then I have more time for the pleasures I want to experience in my life, like reading and spending quality time with my loved ones.

MIHA

Brave Spotlight

* Failing into Success

When privileged and successful, Miha Matlievski, lost everything, he didn't know what to do with himself. Up to that point, everything he ever wanted was handed to him on a silver platter. He was raised to believe success was his birthright. But then it wasn't anymore.

When I interviewed Miha for *The Brave Files* podcast, he was already known as the "Fail Coach." By then Miha had looked into himself deep enough to turn his epic failures into a brand new empire—This time with far more truth and humility. Warmed by his knowledge and experience, Miha now teaches other people that striving for success is harder than striving for spectacular failure because failure is proof that you're trying, learning, and, most importantly, making progress.

Miha's journey started in an unexpected way. He dropped out of high school, believing an education was less important than solid work experience, and went to work at his father's company. He was destined to be the boss of a thriving business, or so he thought. Then, suddenly, his father was diagnosed with cancer and died three weeks later. Things started to go downhill quickly. He was offered the majority shares of his father's business and asked to handle all sales and networking, and others would run the company. Unfortunately, in the end, things didn't turn out as planned.

Miha pivoted to start his own businesses and was especially involved in real estate. He began investing in shopping malls and apartment complexes. Then the real estate market plummeted in the middle of a project and they lost financing. All of his businesses were collateral for the bank, so Miha lost everything. He was left with five million dollars of personal debt and no option for filing bankruptcy. Threats of lawsuits or worse started coming in from the people he owed. He became depressed and experienced severe anxiety and saw no way to climb out of his despair. *So this is it,* he thought. He was an obvious failure. He even considered ending his life by suicide but feared he might even fail at that.

A "perfect childhood" where nobody ever held him accountable for anything wasn't a strong foundation for what was ahead. He'd been a golden child, for goodness sake. Nothing he did was considered wrong by his parents and he lived as a self-proclaimed "king."

It didn't take long before Miha discovered that some basic life skills were missing due to his pampered upbringing. He didn't know how to wake up with an alarm clock or change a light bulb. His parents took responsibility for everything, allowing him to live a carefully-constructed, fun-filled existence that was not sustainable in adulthood or entrepreneurship. Miha became well-versed in blaming all his problems on someone or something else, like the government, the real estate crisis, or politics.

But then something changed. For the first time in his life, he decided to take ownership of his misfortune. And he realized his mistakes had led to massive learning and growth. Perhaps, he thought, a mental shift on "failure" would help put things in perspective. He was learning to fail forward.

Eventually Miha realized that he did have many valuable skills. It was time, he thought, to make a break for personal, mental, and physical liberation, so he started an intentional journey towards personal and business development. Shifting his mindset and approach lead to a completely different experience, both personally and professionally.

The "Fail Coach" was born out of this new realization. He began attending meetups and events that allowed him to meet other entrepreneurs and have insightful conversations. What started as vulnerable, approachable honesty about his story and his failures became the foundation for his business.

When things do not go exactly as planned, we consider them failures. Miha reminds us this is a dangerous mindset. He shares that "When things don't go as you hoped or intended, you're better served to react logically rather than emotionally. Emotions cloud our vision. They strip us of the ability to figure out our mistakes, learn from them, and reach our goals."

This approach of finding the lessons rather than dying from failure is a new concept for many, and it's spot-on. Perceived failure is the number one cause of suicide among entrepreneurs and the fear of failure is the number-one dream killer. Miha maintains that being a Fail Coach doesn't mean that he doesn't fail anymore. In fact, nothing could be farther from the truth. He fails often! But because he now has solid systems in place, he recognizes failure much sooner and he can react and redirect more quickly. Failure makes us step out of our comfort zones, which is necessary for our personal growth. *

Brave Action

Making and Keeping Commitments

When you are intentional about all elements of commitment, you will develop success-related habits. I'm telling you, it feels amazing!

- What are three things you've been holding off on that you can commit right now? Be specific here. If this is a task, assign a specific date and time to it.

- List out any "ways of being" you are committed to for the next week.

- What items do you have the most difficulty committing to? Identify ONE thing you can do to take action on them right now.

- Who do you want to connect with and why? Make a plan to reach out to them (again, be specific).

- What do you want to learn this week and why? How will you make time for it in your schedule?

- Spend ten to fifteen minutes thinking about what's not working in your life. These are likely areas where you've failed to either make strong commitments or follow through. Be honest with yourself!

Un-had Conversations

I try really hard to pay attention to what the Universe is telling me. I find that when I do so, I'm always led in the right direction and, more often than not, come out in a good spot. In the course of the last several years I've been reminded, again and again, how important it is to have conversations with people and about topics that I've put off or avoided. Why? Because these un-had conversations owned a hell of a lot of real-estate in my mind. They kept me up at night and prevented me from being my best, happiest self.

So what is an un-had conversation? It is simply a conversation that you have not had, but wish you would. These conversations can be difficult and they often take a lot of trust and courage—but not always. Un-had conversations can be anything from telling a friend that you're sad because you don't see them often enough to confronting a client who is behind on payment.

How many un-had conversations are eating away at you? Are there things you wish you'd said or done to get something off your chest, ask for (or receive) forgiveness, or avoid regret? If you're anything like me, you've had many moments like that.

The good news is that it's never too late to have these conversations. Yes, it might feel a little awkward if the un-had conversation is years overdue, but you have the power to rewrite the story! I've had conversations with those that have passed by writing a letter and then burning it. In the end, the conversation is about you. It's about releasing any pain, shame, guilt, or regret that is holding you back.

When I first started my blog, I wrote about living without regret. I think this falls in that same category of listening to your inner voice and trusting your gut. A few years ago, I realized that un-had conversations took up way too much space in my mind and my heart. They seemed to take over and put this heavy cloud on everything I did. It was too much and unnecessary. I decided right then and there that I would face situations head on. I would eat the frog. As Mark Twain is often attributed saying, "Eat a live frog every morning and nothing worse will happen to you the rest of the day" (And check out the book *Eat That Frog! 21 Great Ways to Stop Procrastinating and Get More Done in Less Time* by Brian Tracy).

While jumping headfirst into uncomfortable conversations is not my idea of a good time—Neither is sitting with the weight of the un-had conversation. I truly believe that talking things through rather than holding on to them is part of a healthy life balance. For me, designing my life to be balanced in every aspect is a top priority.

Brave Action

Having Hard Conversations

Un-had conversations can weigh heavily on our hearts and minds. I like to say they take up "emotional real estate." Today, I encourage you to ask yourself what un-had conversations are weighing you down? What's possible if you had these conversations? Are you willing to take the plunge and talk it out?

Give yourself the gift of releasing these conversations from your life. Set ten minutes aside to list out what conversations would free you up and release you from additional emotional drain.

When making your list consider these questions:

- How do these un-had conversations make you feel?

- What's the worst thing that could happen if you had this conversation?

- What's the best thing that could happen if you had this conversation?

- How might you feel after you've had the conversation? Think back to the beginning of the book when I asked you to consider how you feel after you complete brave acts!

- Is it worth the risk?

While I encourage you to have all these un-had conversations over time, be brave today and have or schedule just one of the conversations on your list. Commit to a day and time and remember how great you're going to feel on the other side of clearing up that emotional and mental space.

Asking for Feedback is Terrifying and Empowering AF!

There are some words I just can't ever spell correctly. Ever. I love spell check.

I remember when I first entered the workforce as a young, eager event planner for The American Cancer Society. I created and ran the Young Professionals Board of Chicago. It was a hard job but I loved it. I made very little money. In fact, I made so little money that I had two other jobs to keep the bills paid. But I believed in our mission and loved the volunteers I worked with.

When I applied for the job, one of my interview questions was "Will you provide email?" because it was still so new that most companies didn't offer it. There was definitely no such thing as spell check in the email program my office provided. And like I said, I can't spell well.

After being in the job for several months, one of my board members, Bridget, who is a few years older than me, took the time to talk with me about the spelling errors in my emails. She said "You're so smart but the spelling errors totally undermine your authority and knowledge." I remember being fully and completely horrified by this conversation but also eternally grateful. I can't tell you, twenty four years later, how often I revisit that conversation. I could've been hurt or offended by Bridget's comment, but I knew, even then, that she really wanted me to succeed. I knew she was showing how much she cared by providing that constructive criticism. It's important to have people in our lives that care about us enough to tell the truth.

Bridget and I became Facebook friends a few years back and, not that long ago, I thanked her for being brave and caring enough to call me out on my spelling errors. I told her that her actions changed my life. This is a situation I've replayed in my mind countless times and, funnily enough, she didn't even remember doing it. But she shared that someone had done the same for her when she was young and in a new career. When we support one another and show up for one another, it's the most magical thing ever.

The thing is, I didn't even know I was spelling things wrong. Now, every software I use puts big bold squiggly lines underneath my incorrectly-spelled words and I can fix them before sharing them with the public. Of course, autocorrect is my nemesis, and on social media I have errors all the time! I've learned to adjust when I can but to not beat myself up about it. We all make mistakes.

Asking for and giving feedback is one of the most challenging things about adulting, in my opinion. As kids we don't seem bothered by it because we're in a constant state of learning. But eventually we get old enough to think we know everything there is to know. In this stage of life, any negative feedback is an indicator of our faults or failures. Thankfully, most of us eventually evolve into an understanding that feedback is just more information for us to work with. We learn that what other people think of us is, really, none of our business.

Asking for feedback also gives others the opportunity to share positive thoughts as well! We so often associate feedback with the negative, but it isn't always bad!

It's my hope for you that you're always surrounded by people like Bridget. People who want to tell you the truth so you can grow and achieve your dreams. And, equally important, I want you to be that person for others.

We can't build impactful lives and businesses we love by being shy or scared. These things are only accomplished when we are kind but honest and insist on the same from others.

Here are some great ways to ask for feedback:

- "How was that?"

- "What did you think?

- "Was that what you expected?"

- "Was there anything I could have done differently to improve it?"

- "What did you like about this experience?"

Providing feedback is a little different because you want to be clear but kind. One of my clients, Keith, always reminds me to use the sandwich approach when critiquing his work. The sandwich approach is effective because you start with positive feedback, sandwich the critisim in the middle, and close with more positive feedback. For example: "I love the packages you put together here. They're really smart. I'd suggest cleaning up the design a little so it looks as professional as possible. But people are going to love this product!"

When providing feedback it's often helpful to ask questions in the process so that you have a more clear understanding of what the other person was thinking. This is not the time to make assumptions—and you know what they say about assumptions anyway. *They make an ass out of U and Me.*

Providing feedback:

- "What were you hoping to accomplish here?"

- "What are your goals for this?"

- "Why didn't you ask for support?"

- "Why don't we work on this together next time!"

There are no safe spaces, only safe people. It's on you to be a safe person for the people on your team, in your family, and your community. That doesn't mean you should be a doormat! It means you can be trusted to be authentic and honest. Be the person folks can expect kind honesty from.

Make It Bigger Than You!

At the end of each episode of *The Brave Files* podcast I ask my guest what their favorite charitable organization is to support. I typically say something like "I love asking this question because it falls on us, as a global community, to show up for one another. To lift each other up and give what we can. It doesn't have to be money. Time, attention, social media likes—anything counts."

But this isn't just a thing I think. There's actual science behind the notion that when our work and our lives are "bigger than us" there's a positive effect on our overall health. Studies have shown that any act of altruism (that is, a selfless act for others) is connected to positive physical and mental effects. In a study conducted by the Cleveland Clinic, they identified lower blood pressure, increased self-esteem, less depression, lower stress levels, greater overall happiness, and even, in some cases, a longer life.[4]

We create more purpose in our lives simply by thinking about what's important to us, what problem we'd like to be a small part of helping solve, and what opportunities are available for us to volunteer our time and knowledge.

An article by Greater Good Magazine identifies five ways giving is good for us.[5]

1. Giving makes us happy and these good feelings are reflected in our body. The National Institute of Health found that when people give to charities, it activates regions of the brain associated with pleasure, social connection, and trust.[6] All of these combined create a type of "warm glow effect." Scientists who study Positive Psychology also believe that these altruistic behaviors release endorphins in the brain, producing a positive feeling called "helper's high."

2. Giving is good for your health! In his book *Why Good Things Happen to Good People*, Stephen Post, a professor of preventive medicine at Stony Brook University, reports that giving to others has been shown to increase health benefits in people with chronic illness, including HIV and multiple sclerosis. Research indicates that giving may improve physical health and longer life because it helps decrease stress, which is associated with a variety of health problems.[7]

3. Giving promotes cooperation and social connection. Essentially, giving begets giving and those who give are more likely to be given to. This exchange of giving creates a sense of trust, community, and support that strengthens our connections to others. Research has shown that having positive social interactions is key to good mental and physical health. Even more powerful is the proven notion that, when we give to others, they feel closer to us and we feel closer to them.

4. Giving evokes gratitude. Whether you're giving or receiving a gift, you're bound to experience gratitude in some form or fashion. And as I've previously shared, gratitude is integral to happiness, health, and social connection. Dr. Robert Emmons (who was kind enough to allow me to quote him in my books *Shift Your Focus* and *Grow Grateful*) found that

teaching college students to "count their blessings" and cultivate gratitude caused them to exercise more, be more optimistic, and feel better about their lives overall.

5. Giving is contagious. The small act of giving doesn't just affect the person or organization you've given to. It creates a ripple effect of generosity throughout the entire community. A study by James Fowler and Nicholas Christakis published in the *Proceedings of the National Academy of Science* shows that when one person behaves generously, it inspires observers to behave generously towards others. In fact, the researchers found that altruism could spread by three degrees—From person to person to person to person. "As a result," they write, "each person in a network can influence dozens or even hundreds of people, some of whom he or she does not know and has not met."[8]

Giving, it turns out, is linked to the release of oxytocin, a hormone—also released during sex and breastfeeding—that induces feelings of warmth, euphoria, and connection to others. Giving creates more empathy and generosity in ourselves and others.

I have a general rule that I donate to every cause that's presented to me. The amount is usually small, typically around five dollars, but I give what I can to as many fundraising efforts as possible so long as they are in line with my moral compass and personal values. It feels wonderful to support my friends and colleagues in their fundraising efforts and I feel like I'm making a bigger contribution to the world at large. It's a total win-win.

How will you ensure your life is bigger than you?

DHRUV

Brave Spotlight

✳ Empathy Scientist

One of the coolest people I've ever met through podcasting is sixteen-year-old Dhruv Pai.

Dhruv got involved in his middle school community service club because he wanted to make new friends. Since eighth grade, he's volunteered at the local military hospital through the Red Cross during the summer. Being in the volunteering club allowed Dhruv to kill two birds with one stone—He could meet new people and do something he already likes doing: helping people. He never could have imagined what was in store for him once he decided to make his decision "bigger than him."

The pandemic ushered in a profound sense of loneliness, hopelessness, and perhaps uselessness for Dhruv. When his parents suggested that elderly people might need help getting groceries and medicine, Dhruv decided that he could fill that need. Along with a friend, he began a nonprofit called Teens Helping Seniors. They started serving elderly people in their hometown and offered contactless delivery of groceries and medications for seniors, veterans, and the immunocompromised.

The idea of starting a nonprofit at sixteen was daunting. Dhruv understands that community service is most impactful when it's a consistent, intentional commitment. But that requires a level of responsibility and accountability that doesn't come naturally to teenagers (or many adults, period).

Media attention helped evolve Teens Helping Seniors into something bigger than Dhruv and his friends could have dreamed.

When the service was featured by places like *CNN*, *National Public Radio*, and *The Washington Post*, they got messages from people in other communities who expressed interest in beginning their own regional chapter. Now, Teens Helping Seniors offers services across North America. Dhruv doesn't oversee much of what the other chapters do, however. He believes that local leaders understand their community's specific needs better than he could.

Dhruv talks about Teens Helping Seniors with humility. His achievements aren't because he's intrinsically special, he insists, just that he's diligent. He believes empathy is a learned trait that demands practice. Helping out in the community is one way to flex our empathy muscles. When I asked him on *The Brave Files* podcast what he'd like to do professionally, Dhruv said he wants to help design systems for community aid—in his words, become an "empathy scientist."

I'm pretty excited to see a generation of adults who strive to be like Dhruv. These kids are deeply committed to making the world about more than themselves. Imagine it, a global community of empathy scientists. Hope abounds. *

Remember That the Game Changes. Be Ready for It.

The other week, I was chatting with my accountability partner, Eddie. It was our regular call and this one went deep. We started talking about change as the constant and how we needed to roll with the punches.

Eddie asked me how The BRAVE Method helps people deal with change rather than the change knocking them on their asses. I'll admit, I was pretty excited by this question. The BRAVE Method was *made* to help people troubleshoot change. Literally every element of the method is geared towards helping you look at things with fresh eyes, from a different perspective and see how these changes can either work with you or direct you towards a new destination.

All of this to say the only constant is change.

Of course, everything changes—the seasons, our emotions, how busy we are, our connections with friends, how well we care for ourselves, the TV shows we like, the podcasts we listen to, the type of furniture we want to have in our home. Everything.

Everything changes and while change can be terrifying, it's something that, if embraced, has the ability to give you a whole new level of freedom.

I designed my life and business to allow myself to feel good and be present with my family while remaining focused on my business and achieving my goals. You can do the same.

All of these things can happen at once. Designing the life and business you want works if you're willing to put the effort in. If you show up for yourself, don't listen to the bullshit stories in your head, and implement The BRAVE Method you're going to amaze yourself. But you won't amaze me, because I've always known you had it in you.

Making the Invisible, Visible

A couple of years ago, I interviewed a woman named Jennifer S. Royal on *The Brave Files* podcast. Jennifer is a mentalism, mindset, and hypnosis coach. She's also a German-born magician and hypnotist. I don't know about you, but this is all wildly fascinating to me.

During our interview, I excitedly shared with Jennifer that my new book *Gratitude Journal: Shift Your Focus* was to be published that week. And she said, "Heather! You are magic too! You made something that was invisible, visible. You pictured it in your head, and now you are holding it in your hand."

This comment literally stopped me in my tracks. She was right! I'd created something out of nothing. I had manifested this awesome new book. I HAD MADE SOMETHING INVISIBLE BECOME VISIBLE!

I hope you will sit with this idea for a minute. There is so much power and magic in this concept. What have you turned from invisible to visible? What are the possibilities in front of you if you simply consider taking something from your mind and making it a reality? How often do we stand on the edge of our own magic like that?

Since that initial conversation with Jennifer I've made a lot of invisible things visible including a second gratitude book, a fan-freaking-tastic group coaching program (Intentionally Brave Entrepreneurs), the Create Brave manifestation cards, *The Brave Files* Podcast, and this book just to name a few!

But even more importantly, I've used my conversation with Jennifer as an example in hundreds of conversations, be it from the stage, in a coaching call, or in passing conversation, to help other people see the possibilities in front of them.

Here's what I know for sure. You are magic. The real question is, what kind of magic do you want to make? What do you want to take from invisible to visible? And what's stopping you?

My #1 Rule

Even though I've written an entire book guiding you in The BRAVE Method and providing actionable ways to design and create a life you love, I want to leave you with one final thought.

Anyone in my Intentionally Brave Entrepreneurs program can tell you my number one "Brave Rule." They can spout it off like they're in a military lineup.

What's my number one rule, you ask? It's simply that there are no rules.

"I only have one rule and it's that there are no rules!"

This is your life to build. These are your dreams to chase. Your mountains to climb. You get to do them any fucking way you want to, with your fear in tow, your shoulders back, and head held high. It doesn't matter what anyone has done before you or what they will do after you. This is your own, big, bold, beautiful, brave life and there are no fucking rules!

CRYSTAL

Brave Spotlight

✳ Going All In

As an ever-present reminder that what we seek is seeking us, let me tell you about Crystal. In a bit of happenstance and wild luck, Crystal learned about The BRAVE Method Workshops on LinkedIn the day before we kicked off in mid-March 2021. At the time, Crystal found herself in a job (in fact, in an entire *career*) that left her miserable. Although she knew she wanted something different, she had no idea what that actually was. The workshop seemed like as good a place as any to try to understand herself and her future desires a little bit better. She registered and cleared her schedule to attend what was, at the time, a nine-day event.

The BRAVE Method Workshop is a hands-on, intensive experience. I, along with other members of my team, teach The BRAVE Method and show how it can be applied in any circumstance. And then we ask our attendees to dig in for themselves with the workbook we provide. This workbook is filled with thought-provoking questions to help you get really clear on what you want, why you want it, and how to get it. Although these questions look really innocent and simple, they're anything but. If you actually show up with the intention to grow and change and you take the homework seriously, you'll learn magical things about yourself and start to envision a life and a future that you are passionately in love with. The workbook is much like the Brave Action prompts in this very book. Should you choose to apply yourself and really dig in, I can guarantee that things will shift for you in a very significant way. Your self-awareness will strengthen, your truest desires will become more clear, and a path towards whatever success you seek will present itself.

So, let's go back to that day in March. Crystal dove headfirst into the workbook. On the first day, she identified that if she stayed at her current job she wouldn't be happy but it would pay off her debt. It was, after all, a good six-figure job. And then she got to the question that changed everything: "If you could change anything, what would you do?" Her answer surprised her. "If I could do anything," she wrote, "I'd be a lawyer. I'd work for myself and be in control of what issues and who I devote my time to." She started to imagine what was possible if she quit her job, studied for the LSAT, and got into law school.

Then, three days later, she was laid off from her job and offered a generous severance package. This was the opportunity she'd been waiting for! At that moment, Crystal made some life-altering decisions. She would join Intentionally Brave Entrepreneurs, get her mediators certification, take the LSAT, and apply to law school.

Within a couple of months, she got into law school and was finishing up her North Carolina Supreme Court Mediators Certification, putting her five years ahead of the rest of her law school class. There's now a clear picture of the business she plans to one day open as an International Mediation and Arbitration Firm. In the course of just a few short months, at the age of 44, Crystal went from unenergized and apathetic about her life to imagining her wildest dreams and being well on her way to making them a reality.

I recently invited Crystal to speak at a new session of the workshop. She shared with the audience how The BRAVE Method completely altered her life. A few times she considered backing down and going to work for someone else, but through her work with the Three R's—digging deep into reassessment, reframing, and resilience—she *knew* that working for someone else was not going to make her happy. She decided to stay the course, trust The BRAVE Method, trust herself, and trust the process. "All of this," Crystal tells us, "is possible through my work with IBE and The BRAVE Method. I revisit every element of The BRAVE Method all the time. I find that for me to be my most empowered, authentic self and to truly lean into that realm of possibility, I have to go back and see where I was before and how I've grown. *Everything is possible.*"

Now Crystal gives herself permission to expand into her dreams and empower herself. Every single day, she asks herself what is possible. She fully embraces a gratitude practice that opened her eyes to so much more creativity, connectivity, and opportunity. "I know this program works because I live it every single day," she says. Crystal is living proof that The BRAVE Method works. If you show up for yourself and go all in, literally anything is possible. ✳

Acknowledgments and Thanks

Writing a book is a mighty effort and it's one that's never done alone! None of this would have been possible without these people—and Dear Universe, I hope I didn't forget anyone!

It takes a special person with a generous and open heart to be a beta reader. I asked these readers to look past the messy first draft, the typos, the mistakes, and really see this book with their hearts. Each beta reader gave me comfort and confidence as they, one by one, assured me it was a wonderful and worthwhile book. Thank you, from the bottom of my heart, to Jennifer Archer, Nicole Cattan, Sabrina DelMonaco, Nicole Durkin, Mary Fields, Barbie Hull, Angela Locashio, Manuella Powell, Annie P. Ruggles, and Pamela Stamper. To Boomer Lowe, thanks for stepping in at the last minute to read, review and give me your honest feedback. And, Team BRAVE—what would I do without you? Thank you for making it all work.

A book is only as good as its editing and design and for this, I am wildly grateful to Ali Chambers for her effervescent lust for life, her enthusiasm for this book, and for making the editing process feel like a treat rather than a chore. I am so, so grateful that the cosmos brought us together. Sabrina DelMonaco, whose attention to every single tiny detail helped ensure I didn't fuck anything up. Lee Lee McKnight for ensuring all of the proper sources were cited and your detailed proof reading. Jessie Leiber, my outstanding cover artist and layout designer, you've been on this journey with me for so many years now that I couldn't possibly do it without you—And more to the point, I wouldn't want to! Thank you for taking my ideas and making them visually beautiful. Your creative approach never ceases to leave me giddy with excitement. You can kind of see inside my brain, and that's cool.

To all of my wonderful, amazing, brilliant clients across the years and those still to come. Thank you for trusting me and helping me bring The BRAVE Method out into the world in real and exciting ways. Supporting you is the greatest gift and I am humbled beyond words. It is my life's pleasure to be on the journey with you. Special thanks to the clients and podcast guests who I've featured in this book. Thank you for allowing me to share your stories! You're all such wonderful inspirations and I am so grateful to know you.

Personal Thanks

I'd like to insert a grand gesture here because words don't seem good enough, but I don't know what *could* possibly be good enough. So I hope you feel my words of gratitude and thanks to your very core.

Neda Ward, Momma. Thank you for being my first and most fervent cheerleader. You taught me to always fight for what I wanted, never take no for an answer, and to lead with love, no matter what. I hope I've made you proud.

Doris Forester, Granny. I'm sometimes amazed at how your wisdom reaches me from the beyond and I'm sorry we never got to talk about it together when you were on this side. I feel you with me always and I'm paying attention. Thank you for the best gift ever.

Olivia, Eve, Tessa, and Scarlett, my extraordinary daughters. All things are for you. Always. There's nothing you can't do if you put your mind to it. Remember this, even on the hard days (perhaps especially on the hard days)—You are worthy, valued, loved, and Brave AF. Being your mother is my greatest gift and my proudest accomplishment. Mostly, I love that you exist as your honest, authentic, and spectacular selves without apology. I am so grateful I get the privilege of being your mother.

Bernadette Smith, my partner. The ways in which my life has shifted since you entered it are staggering. Your unwavering belief in my ability to be and do literally anything has inspired and encouraged me in ways that I'm not sure I can ever express. I love being the lesbian Will and Jada with you.

Eddie Babbage, my accountability partner. My dear Eddie, who knew that having crossed paths with you would be so life-altering. The depths to which I am grateful for your friendship are so deep and wide I'm not sure I could ever properly express them. Thank you for the countless calls and texts and your endless, wonderful friendship. I can't wait until we write our book together. I'm especially excited to see you on the cover in your purple velvet suit. We make big dreams happen, my friend.

My longtime friend, Keith. It only feels right to give you some extra love here. Because when I look back at my career, the ebbs and flows, the trials and errors, there is only one person that has shown up for every moment as a cheerleader, client, and contributor. You have shown up for every version of my business from that very first workshop to 1:1 coaching, audio courses, small group coaching, flying access country to attend keynote presentations, and being a valued member of IBE. You have seen me try and fail, try again, and get it right. Your love, honesty, and support has meant more than you can ever imagine. You make me laugh and I'd show up early to the airport for you anytime. Thanks for being my buddy.

And finally, *to you*, the person who picked up this book and decided to give it a try. Whether you take The BRAVE Method and run with it or you pick and choose the elements that best work for you, I am grateful and honored. You are going to bring so much magic into the world. Thank you!

References & Resources

Introduction

[1] Van Gogh, Vincent. Vincent Van Gogh to Theo van Gogh, October 28, 1883. From the Van Gogh Museum, *Vincent Van Gogh: The Letters.* http://www.vangoghletters.org/vg/letters/let400/letter.html (accessed November 2020).

[2] Miranda, Lin Manuel. "Yorktown (The World Turned Upside Down)," Track 20 on *Hamilton (Original Broadway Cast Recording).* Atlantic Recording Corporation, digital audio player.

[3] Anastasi, Aaron. *Your Prosperous Mind.* New Dreamers Publishing, 2017.

[4] Gracey, Michael, dir. P!NK: *All I Know So Far.* 2021; Seattle, WA: Amazon Video. Streaming Film.

[5] Vickery, Heather. "survey results." Testimonials. Vickery and Co, 2017. https://bit.ly/37peH8P.

[6] Cameron, Sara. "How to turn busy into balance." TEDxTemecula. January 2, 2016. Video. https://youtu.be/ II_Qyf0Vw9g.

PART 1 (THE BRAVE METHOD BREAKDOWN)

[1] "survey results."

[2] Anastasi, *Your Prosperous Mind.*

[3] Maraboli, Steve. *Life, the Truth, and Being Free.* New York: A Better Today Publishing, 999.

[4] Duckworth, Angela. "Don't Believe the Hype About Grit, Pleads the Scientist Behind the Concept." By Melissa Dahl. The Cut, May 19, 2016.

[5] Duckworth, Angela. "Grit: The Power of Passion and Perseverance." TED: Ideas Worth Exploring. April 2013. https:// www.ted.com/talks/angela_lee_duckworth_grit_the_power_of_ passion_and_perseverace?utm_campaign=tedspread&utm_medi-um=referral&utm_source=tedcomshare.

[6] "VIA Character Strengths Survey & Character Reports." VIA: Institute on Character. Accessed November 2020. https://www. viacharacter.org/.

[7] "VIA Character Strengths Survey & Character Reports."

[8] Brown, Brené. *Braving the Wilderness: The Quest for True Belonging and the Courage to Stand Alone.* New York: Random House. 2017.

PART 2 (MAKING IT HAPPEN)

1 Duhigg, Charles. *The Power of Habit*. New York: Random House, 2014.

2 Rhoades, Heather. "Fall Leaf Life Cycle: Why Do Leaves Change Colors In The Autumn" Gardening Know How. Last modified April 8, 2021. https://www.gardeningknowhow.com/ornamental/trees/tgen/fall-leaf-life-cycle-why-do-leaves-change-colors-in-the-autumn.htm.

3 "Cool autumn weather reveals nature's true hues." National Oceanic and Atmospheric Administration (NOAA). October 1, 2014. https://www.noaa.gov/stories/cool-autumn-weather-reveals-nature-s-true-hues.

PART 3 (KEEP THE MOMENTUM)

1 Winfrey, Oprah. *What I Know For Sure*. New York: Flatiron Books, 2014.

2 Tello, Monique. "A positive mindset can help your heart." Heart Health. *Harvard Health Publishing*. February 14, 2019. https://www.health.harvard.edu/blog/a-positive-mindset-can-help-your-heart-2019021415999.

3 "Gracey, *All I Know So Far*.

4 Sinek, Simon. "How Great Leaders Inspire Action." TEDxPuget Sound. *TED*. September 2009. https://www.ted.com/talks/simon_sinek_how_great_leaders_inspire_action?language=en.

4 Hyman, Mark. "Gratitude Can Boost Your Health: 5 Ways to Develop It." HealthEssentials. *Cleveland Clinic*, February 15, 2018. https://health.clevelandclinic.org/gratitude-can-boost-your-health-5-ways-to-develop-it/.

5 "Suttie, Jill, and Jason Marsh. "5 Ways Giving Is Good for You." Mind & Body. *Greater Good Magazine*, December

13, 2010. https://greatergood.berkeley.edu/article/item/5_ways_giving_is_good_for_you.

[6] Contie, Vicki. "Brain Imaging Reveals Joys of Giving." NIH Research Matters. *National Institutes of Health,* June 22, 2007. https://www.nih.gov/news-events/nih-research-matters/brain-imaging-reveals-joys-giving.

[7] Post, Stephen, and Jill Neimark. *Why Good Things Happen to Good People.* New York: Broadway Books, 2008.

[8] Fowler, James H., and Nicholas A. Christakis. "Cooperative behavior cascades in human social networks." *Proceedings of the National Academy of Science* 107, no. 12 (2010), accessed November 2020, https://doi.org/10.1073/pnas.0913149107.

The Brave Files Podcast episodes featured as Brave Spotlights

- Sarah: #23 "Living Intentionally on Purpose"
- Pasha: #158 "Healing Through Humor"
- Khim: #4 "Proof of Life"
- Tom: #37 "Still Brave"
- Anoushé: #74 "Breaking the Mold"
- Maxwell: #85 "Learning to be Flexible."
- Arlan: #112 "History Making, Industry Changing"
- Alexia: #107 "Own Your Moxie"
- Carla: #96 "Transformation Crash Course"
- Karen: #139 "From Surviving to Thriving: Breaking the Time Barrier"
- Saundra: #76 "The Gifts of Rest"
- Alua: #40 "Death Brought Me Back To Life"
- Trish: #87 "America's First Transgender Infantryman"

- Paige: #91 "Joy Changes Lives"
- Amy: #127 "Check Your Comfort Zone at the Door"
- Miha: #128 "Failure: Your Path to Success"
- Dhruv: #157 "Empathy Scientist: How One Teenager Can Change the World"
- Jennifer: #57 "Magic Mindset"

Gratitude Episodes, *The Brave Files*
- #90: "Growing Grateful Together"
- #109: "Gratitude During Shelter in Place"
- #147: "Grateful Endings and New Beginnings"

Additional Reading Suggestions
- *Leadership and Self-Deception: Getting Out of the Box* by **Arbinger Institute**
- *Braving the Wilderness: The Quest for True Belonging and the Courage to Stand Alone* by **Brené Brown**
- *The Art of Possibility* by **Rosamund Stone Zander and Benjamin Zander**
- *Outliers: The Story of Success* by **Malcolm Gladwell**
- *Grit: The Power of Passion and Perseverance* by **Angela Duckworth**
- *Self-Compassion: The Proven Power of Being Kind to Yourself* by **Dr. Kristen Neff**
- *Failing Up: How to Take Risks, Aim Higher, and Never Stop Learning* by **Leslie Odom, Jr.**
- *The Choice: Embrace The Possible* by **Edith Eager**
- *Year of Yes* by **Shonda Rhimes**
- *Authentic Happiness: Using the New Positive Psychology to Realize Your Potential for Lasting Fulfillment* by **Martin E. P. Seligman**

- *Outrageous Openness: Letting the Divine Take the Lead* **by Tosha Silver**
- *Eat That Frog! 21 Great Ways to Stop Procrastinating and Get More Done in Less Time* **by Brian Tracey**
- *The Power of Habit: Why We do What We Do In Life and Business* **by Charles Duhigg**
- *Wolfpack: How to Come Together, Unleash Our Power, and Change the Game* **by Abby Wambach**

Heather's Gratitude Journals

- *Gratitude Journal: Shift Your Focus*
- *Grow Grateful: A Gratitude Journal for Kids and Families*

Find a full list of suggested reading at: www.vickeryandco.com/books

GET TO WORK!

Download your complete guide to getting started with The BRAVE Method today at: www.vickeryandco.com/TheBraveMethodWorkbook.

Join The Brave on Purpose Collective today and begin making the brave leap with a kickass community of brave leaders just like you. www.vickeryandco.com/BraveOnPurpose